How to Write Essays for Standardized Tests

The Staff of the Princeton Review

PrincetonReview.com

The Princeton Review
110 East 42nd St, 7th Floor
New York, NY 10017

Published in the United States by Penguin Random House, LLC,
New York, and in Canada by Random House of Canada, division
of Penguin Random House Ltd., Toronto.

ISBN: 978-0-525-57153-7
eBook ISBN: 978-0-525-57191-9
ISSN: 2767-729X

Editor: Aaron Riccio
Production Editors: Liz Dacey and Sarah Litt
Production Artist: Deborah Weber

Printed in the United States of America.

10 9 8 7 6 5 4 3 2 1

1st Edition

Editorial
Rob Franek, Editor-in-Chief
David Soto, Director of Content Development
Stephen Koch, Student Survey Manager
Deborah Weber, Director of Production
Jason Ullmeyer, Production Design Manager
Selena Coppock, Director of Editorial
Aaron Riccio, Senior Editor
Meave Shelton, Senior Editor
Chris Chimera, Editor
Anna Goodlett, Editor
Eleanor Green, Editor
Orion McBean, Editor
Patricia Murphy, Editorial Assistant

Penguin Random House Publishing Team
Tom Russell, VP, Publisher
Alison Stoltzfus, Publishing Director
Brett Wright, Senior Editor
Amanda Yee, Associate Managing Editor
Ellen Reed, Production Manager
Suzanne Lee, Designer
Eugenia Lo, Publishing Assistant

For customer service, please contact
editorialsupport@review.com,
and be sure to include:

- full title of the book

- ISBN

- page number

Acknowledgments

The Princeton Review would like to thank Sara Kuperstein, Jess Thomas, and Gabby Budzon for their work in putting together this book. Additional gratitude for the contributions of Chris Benson, Shaina Walter Bowie, Kenneth M. Brenner, Lori DesRochers, Gina Donegan, Anne Goldberg-Baldwin, Sarah Kass, Ali Landreau, Jennifer A. McDevitt, Amy Minster, Jason Morgan, Amanda Nowotny, Danielle Perrini, Stephen Shuck, and Cynthia Ward.

The Princeton Review also appreciates the work done by Debbie Weber in designing and laying out this title, Aaron Riccio for helping to develop and maintain the style, and Liz Dacey and Sarah Litt for their attention to accuracy and details in production.

Contents

Get More
(Free) Content
at PrincetonReview.com/prep

As easy as 1•2•3

1 Go to PrincetonReview.com/prep or scan the **QR code** and enter the following ISBN for your book: **9780525571537**

2 Answer a few simple questions to set up an exclusive Princeton Review account. *(If you already have one, you can just log in.)*

3 Enjoy access to your **FREE** content!

Once you've registered, you can...

- Get valuable advice about the college application process, including tips for applying for financial aid

- Check to see if there have been any corrections or updates to this edition

Need to report a potential **content** issue?

Contact **EditorialSupport@review.com** and include:

- full title of the book
- ISBN
- page number

Need to report a **technical** issue?

Contact **TPRStudentTech@review.com** and provide:

- your full name
- email address used to register the book
- full book title and ISBN
- Operating system (Mac/PC) and browser (Firefox, Safari, etc.)

Introduction

You've likely written many essays in your life, from ones that are just a single paragraph long to those that are dozens of pages in length. Most of your writing has probably been for school—you know the material, you know the grader, and you typically have more than an hour (often days, weeks, months, or even years!) to write. Essays for standardized tests are similar in some respects, but different in many other ways. The writing skills that you have learned in school will be very helpful, but they may not be enough when it comes to some of the particular skills that are needed for standardized test essays. This book will help you conquer these essays and achieve top marks.

WHAT MAKES WRITING FOR STANDARDIZED TESTS DIFFERENT FROM WRITING FOR SCHOOL

What makes for good writing for school assignments? Well, it depends on a lot of factors. Different courses will have different aims, so the grader will focus on different aspects. For instance, a lab report needs to follow a specific structure. The writing needs to be detailed and exhaustive. The lab report shouldn't be written like a novel—a writing style that would be successful in a creative writing course won't work here! Grammar should be correct (to make the writing clear), but the grader's goal isn't to evaluate how well you understand the mechanics of the language.

In contrast, writing for a foreign language class is all about the mechanics. Grammatical rules must be followed—the grader will be looking for those mistakes. Additionally, idiomatic expressions are essential: is the writing like that of a native speaker, or are there borrowings from English (or whatever other language the author speaks or writes)?

As a result, every class and subject has its own requirements. What's successful in one class won't necessarily work in another, especially since the requirements and preferences depend on the grader. Some may want to see writing that gets directly to the point, and others may want to see more of an overview of the thought process. You might have a grader who gives the benefit of the doubt if it seems clear that the student knows the material; then again, you might also have one who channels their disappointment into your grade.

So, what makes writing for standardized tests different? Well, a lot of the above is still true. Different essays will have different requirements, so what is necessary for success on one exam may not be helpful on other exams. Although the grader is some anonymous employee of the test company, there are some things we know about these folks, so we can learn to give them what they're looking for.

The biggest difference between writing for school and writing for standardized tests is time. Most teachers will give an hour or more for an in-class writing assignment, and, of course, essays written outside of school can take many, many hours to write. By contrast, most of the essays in this book give students about 45 minutes (or less) to read and understand the prompt, plan out their essays, actually write, and proofread. The good news is that although you may not know exactly what your essay prompt will be, there is actually a lot of planning that you can do in advance. The more you do to prepare before test day, the easier the writing process will be, and the better your essay will be. In this book, you'll learn the skills that are needed for each essay test you are taking, and you'll develop a solid plan for how to approach any prompt you may be given.

HOW TO USE THIS BOOK

In the first section of this book, you'll find scoring rubrics and samples for many of the essays found on the APs, ACT, SSAT, ISEE, and TOEFL. This will give you a sense of what the graders are looking for and, consequently, what your essay should look like. These are not intended to be perfect samples—rather, they are meant to demonstrate a range of student writing so that you know what to focus on in your own work. Additionally, because we're focusing on writing skills instead of academic content, the prompts have been omitted. If you're looking for sample prompts, you can find them on each test-maker's website, or check out practice tests in our Prep books, which you can find at www.randomhouse.com/princetonreview.

> With limited exceptions—School Day administrations—the SAT no longer offers an essay section. Because most students won't have this option and it is not a college requirement, this book does not cover it.

The second section of this book contains the overall skills and strategies that you'll need to know when it comes time to write your essay. The opening of each chapter tells you which essays the given technique applies to so that you can focus on those most relevant to the test(s) you're preparing for.

THE BIGGER PICTURE

Although this book focuses on specific essay exams, you may find that the skill-related advice helps on other essays. Most essays you have to write for school or for other standardized tests, such as state graduation exams or International Baccalaureate exams, will use many of the same skills we cover in this book. If you will be taking the School Day SAT with essay, the Rhetorical Analysis chapter will give you some great strategies. The Personal Essays chapter may even help with essays you write for college admissions, private high school admissions, or scholarship applications. Many of the tips and techniques in the Long Essay Approaches chapter will apply to just about any essay you write, even those without a time limit. We've kept most of our advice general, in order to apply to multiple tests, so we think you'll find it extremely helpful for much of the writing you have to do.

PART A

TEST INDEX

HOW TO USE THE TEST INDEX

This section of the book generally includes the time limit, the scoring range, a brief description, a rubric, and a sample essay for each essay for the tests included in this book. You'll also be given the relevant skills for each essay, which correspond to the chapters in the second part of this book. After you have read through the information and the sample essay, use that list of chapters to learn the skills that are required for your essay. We did not include sample essays for short-answer questions, as those are scored almost solely on the content rather than the structure of the essay; however, you will find examples and strategies for short-answer questions in the Short Answer Approaches chapter.

Holistic Rubrics

In this section, you'll find some rubrics that give you a certain number of points for fulfilling each scoring area. You'll also see some tests that are scored holistically, which means that the grader gives your essay an overall score based on a variety of areas. We'll let you know the qualities of an adequate essay, one that meets all the criteria; assume that an essay that would score below that is missing one or more of the criteria, and an essay that would earn a higher-than-adequate score goes above and beyond by having more detail, more skillful use of language, and/or more sophistication.

Sample Essays

The sample essays in this section are designed to be one step above adequate; these essays will generally have everything you need, so they should be useful examples for you to emulate. As stated above, essays that would score above the examples in this book would be similar but more elaborate and sophisticated.

A Few Notes

The rubrics in this section are based on the most recently available information, but you may see some variation, especially for AP Exams. For instance, in 2021 some AP Exams offered an alternative online version of the test with a different format and rubric; at the time of this book's publication, it is unknown whether this option will continue in the future and, if it does, what those versions will look like. Furthermore, the maximum number of points for some of the AP Exam essays varies from year to year depending on the prompt that is given, so those scoring ranges and rubrics are approximations. The overall skills that are tested are the same, but we encourage you to find the document called "Course and Exam Description" on the AP website (apcentral.collegeboard.org) for your AP Exam, as this document is regularly revised and will have the most up-to-date information for the year you will be taking your exam.

Chapter 1

History and Government
AP Exams

AP ART HISTORY

Question 1: Comparison Essay

Suggested Time: 35 minutes (out of 120 minutes total)

Scoring Range: 0–8 points

Description: This long essay will ask you to compare a required work of art and another of your choosing and explain the significance of those similarities or differences. This essay will include images of works of art.

RUBRIC		
# of Points Available		**How to Earn Points**
1	**A**	Select and identify another work of art from the same region or time period that depicts the same theme or topic as the required work. *The student must accurately include at least two of the following identifiers for the chosen work: title or designation, name of artist and/or cultural origin, date of creation, and materials.*
1	**B**	Accurately describe the relationship, subject matter, or representation of the required work using specific visual evidence.
1	**C**	Accurately describe the relationship, subject matter, or representation of the chosen work using specific visual evidence.
2	**D**	Accurately describe two similarities or differences between how the required work and chosen work present the subject matter, theme, and/or relationships in the works.
2	**E**	Accurately use at least one piece of specific visual or contextual evidence from each work to support an explanation of each similarity or difference.

Note that this rubric is an approximation, as the points awarded will vary depending on the specific requirements of the prompt.

Relevant Skills for Comparison Essay:

>> General Advice, **see Chapter 4**
>> Long Essay Approaches, **see Chapter 6**
>> Analyzing Quantitative and Graphical Content, **see Chapter 8**
>> Adding Outside Content, **see Chapter 10**
>> Synthesis, **see Chapter 12**

Sample Essay

The prompt for this essay provided an image of a battle scene and asked students to identify another work showing a battle or conflict, such as those in a list provided. In addition to the criteria mentioned in the example rubric above, this prompt instructed students to explain a similarity between the two works related to reinforcing power and leadership concepts.

Another work of art that shows conflict or battle is the Column of Trajan in Rome, Italy. In this battle scene from the Great Altar of Zeus, gods and other powerful beings such as giants are shown waging war to decide who will control the universe. Athena is portrayed in the center, pulling a strong, winged being by the hair as she defeats him. Another winged being flies into view to crown Athena the winner of the fight, and a woman looks on in fear of the whole battle. These images show the power of the gods and indicate that Athena has become the slayer of the giants. The imagery of the Column of Trajan shows the war between the Romans and the Dacians, waged by Emperor Trajan and his army. The lower half depicts the first major victory against the Dacians. The upper half shows the second victorious campaign by the Roman army. Other scenes on the column spiral frieze show troops preparing and leaving for battle and military leaders giving speeches, indicating the war's focus on expansion and the conquest of Dacia.

A

Does not get this point, as there is only one identifier here (title does not count, as it was provided). Would get the point if the culture, materials, or date were also given accurately.

B

Uses specific visual evidence to describe the given work

C

Uses specific visual evidence to describe the chosen work

One similarity in the way these works show battle or conflict is the imagery used to show the victors of the battles. Both works show the victors as strong, powerful, and in control, while the enemy is not organized or capable. For the Great Altar at Pergamon, the giant that Athena grabs in her hands is lower in the image, twisted and unable to move, while she is above him, standing in a powerful pose of victory. The central image of Athena shows her importance to the Greeks as the goddess of wisdom and war, further indicated by her crowning at the moment of victory. The entire Column of Trajan is a monument to his victory over the Dacians, with his ashes in the base to emphasize his legacy. The recurring images of the emperor and military leaders show their belief in his power and add weight to his importance. The enemy, though, is not shown in such a positive light, with the base of the column covered in the weapons and armor of the defeated soldiers.

Provides a similarity and explains it using specific visual details

One difference between the Great Altar and the Column of Trajan is the portrayal of the actual fighting. In the Great Altar, a single moment in what was a long and complex battle is shown, focusing the viewer's attention on only the moment of victory. This moment is further emphasized by the high relief of the frieze and the intense poses of the figures, making the win even more dramatic. The Column of Trajan, on the other hand, shows many scenes from throughout the two wars it covers. These scenes are in low relief, and they tell of several aspects of the wars as the frieze spirals around the column. Furthermore, the scenes focus more on preparation for war, military leadership, and the role of the emperor in overseeing the military.

Presents and explains a difference and uses specific visual details in the body paragraph

Both works, though they have different approaches, convey similar ideas about the role of the divine in battle. The emperor Trajan himself led the wars against the Dacians, and the Column celebrates not only his victories but also the greatness of the emperor who oversaw them. The gods themselves fought the battle in the Great Altar scene, with Athena defeating the giants with her great power. The drama and the contrast of the work demonstrate the power of the gods and the reverence shown to them.

This essay wouldn't earn the additional point for the reference to power and leadership concepts, as that isn't fully explained here

Question 2: Visual/Contextual Analysis Essay

Suggested Time: 25 minutes (out of 120 minutes total)

Scoring Range: 0–6 points

Description: This long essay will ask you to select and identify a work of art and make assertions about it based on evidence. No images are provided.

# of Points Available		How to Earn Points
		RUBRIC
1	**A**	Select and identify a work of art from a specific time period and/or region that utilized specific materials, techniques, or details to convey a subject matter or theme. *The student must accurately include at least two of the following identifiers for the chosen work: title or designation, name of artist and/or cultural origin, date of creation, and materials.*
2	**B**	Accurately describe two materials, techniques, or details used to convey the subject matter or theme.
1	**C**	Accurately explain the commentary on the subject matter that the artist intended to make through his or her use of these materials and techniques.
2	**D**	Accurately use two pieces of specific visual or contextual evidence to support the explanation.

Relevant Skills for Visual/Contextual Analysis Essay:

>> General Advice, **see Chapter 4**
>> Long Essay Approaches, **see Chapter 6**
>> Adding Outside Content, **see Chapter 10**

Sample Essay

The prompt for this essay asked students to select and identify a work of art, such as one in a list provided, and explain how a depiction of the natural world is used to communicate a political or social statement.

A

Provides two identifiers besides the title, which had been provided: artist's name and approximate date

The Oxbow by Thomas Cole is an oil painting on canvas from the early 19th century. The landscape painting shows a scene of a river winding through a valley, just after a thunderstorm. Visually, the painting is divided by a diagonal line going from the upper left to the lower right side, with greenery and trees on the left and the river and farmlands on the right.

Specific visual details

B

Another piece of visual evidence

The two halves are very different from each other. On the left, the trees look wild, with lots of green leaves and twisty roots and branches. The farmlands on the right, in contrast, are flat, dull, and orderly, with even the river creating a gentle loop with a smooth surface. Cole was interested in showing the beauty of America and used his paintings to create pride in the viewer about the majesty of the landscape. He knew that America had a unique beauty all its own, which he elevated with his work by showing the variety and contrast in this scene.

D

Uses specific visual context to explain why the artist depicted it this way

C

Explains the artist's intended commentary

Cole also included an image of himself in the scene. The figure witnesses the change in weather and the grand scenery around him. Since the artist is both the creator and the observer in the painting, Cole suggests a duality in terms of his participation in the scene. The contrast between the two halves of the painting correspond with this duality of the artist.

Another piece of visual evidence that supports the explanation

Concluding sentence ties together the points made

Questions 3–6: Short Essays

Suggested Time: 15 minutes each (out of 120 minutes total)

Scoring Range: 0–5 points for each short essay

Description: You'll be asked to analyze the provided sources, analyze historical developments and processes described in the sources, put those historical developments and processes in context, and make connections between those historical developments and processes.

❑ One Visual Analysis will ask you to describe a work of art beyond the image set and connect it to an artistic tradition, style, or practice.

❑ One Contextual Analysis will ask you to describe contextual influences of a work of art in the image set and explain how context can influence artistic decisions.

❑ One Attribution will ask you to attribute a work of art beyond the image set to a particular artist, culture, or style, and justify your assertions with evidence.

❑ One Continuity and Change will ask you to analyze the relationship between a provided work of art and a related artistic tradition, style, or practice.

❑ All four short essay prompts will include images of works of art.

RUBRIC
How to Earn Points
The prompt for each question will list five tasks. You'll earn a point for each task that you complete correctly.

Relevant Skills for Short Essays:

» General Advice, **see Chapter 4**
» Short Answer Approaches, **see Chapter 5**
» Analyzing Quantitative and Graphical Content, **see Chapter 8**

AP COMPARATIVE GOVERNMENT AND POLITICS

Questions 1–3: Short Answer

Suggested Time: 10–20 minutes each (out of 90 minutes total)

Scoring Range: 0–4 or 0–5 points for each short essay

Description:

❑ One Conceptual Analysis will ask you to define or describe a political concept and explain and/or compare political systems, principles, institutions, processes, policies, or behaviors.

❑ One Quantitative Analysis will provide quantitative information (a graph, map, table, or infographic) and ask you to describe the data, connect it to course concepts, and draw a conclusion.

❑ One Comparative Analysis will ask you to compare political concepts, systems, institutions, processes, or policies in two of the course countries.

RUBRIC
How to Earn Points
The prompt will provide 4–5 tasks for each short-answer question. You'll earn a point for each task that is completed correctly.

Relevant Skills for Short Answer:

» General Advice, **see Chapter 4**
» Short Answer Approaches, **see Chapter 5**
» Analyzing Quantitative and Graphical Content, **see Chapter 8**

Question 4: Argument Essay

Suggested Time: 40 minutes (out of 90 minutes total)

Scoring Range: 0–5 points

Description: You'll write an evidence-based essay supporting a claim or thesis related to course concepts and course countries.

# of Points Available		How to Earn Points
RUBRIC		
1	**A**	Respond to the prompt with a defensible claim or thesis that establishes a line of reasoning. *The thesis may be one or more sentences, anywhere in the essay.*
2	**B**	Provide two pieces of specific and relevant evidence from one or more course countries relevant to one or more of the course concepts in the prompt.
1	**C**	Explain how or why the evidence supports the claim or thesis.
1	**D**	Respond to an opposing or alternate perspective using refutation, concession, or rebuttal.

Relevant Skills for Argument Essay:

» General Advice, **see Chapter 4**
» Long Essay Approaches, **see Chapter 6**
» Adding Outside Content, **see Chapter 10**
» Argumentative Essays, **see Chapter 13**

Sample Essay

The prompt for this essay asked whether authoritarianism is growing in strength around the world and asked students to use one or more of the given countries as examples.

Many people fear that authoritarianism, which is characterized by a very strong central power and limited personal freedoms, has been growing as some political leaders around the world have turned to this form of government, shying away from democracy. It seems as if the news is constantly covering stories about the proliferation of authoritarianism, from Brazil to Russia. However, plenty of people still oppose this type of regime. Using historical examples of events in Russia and Iran, this essay will argue that although some countries have adopted authoritarian styles in recent decades, opposition to authoritarianism among constituents of this type of political system may ultimately hinder its growth.

Russia had its first taste of democracy in the 1990s, just after the communist system, which demonstrated many elements of authoritarianism, had fallen. In 1991, Boris Yeltsin was elected in the country's very first presidential elections, and he brought democracy to his people. During this decade, Russia gained a new reputation, and people in the West considered in investing money in the nation. But this period didn't last long. A few years later, Vladimir Putin, former head of the national security department that succeeded the old KGB, arrived and soon entered the picture. Before long, he'd usurped a lot of power in the same type of way that the old communist leaders had done. Putin made a few people in the country very rich, establishing an oligarchy. Putin remains in power, but many Russians oppose him and his authoritarian rule. Anti-authoritarian movements have gained momentum throughout country over the last few decades. Musical groups like Pussy Riot, which emerged in the 2000s, have protested Putin's power seizing. More recently, in 2021, Russian citizens have been mobilizing to protest Putin's reign. Russians outside the country have spoken out against this authoritarianism as well, even at the expense of their lives. While Putin and authoritarianism remain in Russia, a shift to democracy might be just around the corner.

Authoritarian systems can emerge anywhere and take on many forms. Iran's current political system is theocracy, which views a deity as the ultimate sovereign power, that is rooted in authoritarianism. Many of the state's policies and laws are based on tradition, too. Iran emerged as a theocracy in 1979, when the former ruler, the shah, was overthrown (against the wishes of the CIA). Since then, the leader of the government, the ayatollah, has ruled the country together with

Clear definition of central term at the onset of the essay

B Good integration of facts and historical backdrop in this paragraph

D Clear transition away from the counter-argument and into the main argument

A Thesis is clear and establishes the reasoning that will be used

Defines the term oligarchy

Clear definition of theocracy

 B Good use of historical backdrop of Iranian revolution

the mullahs, and they have jailed anybody who disagrees with them, especially journalists. Such extremism has been criticized by democracies. Moreover, Iran has been ostracized by other authoritarian Middle Eastern countries because of its nuclear weapons program, and because these other countries don't seem to trust the ayatollah. Meanwhile, as in the case of Russia, there have been many protests against the Iranian religious authoritarian regime. There was a strongly disputed election in 2009, and since then, there has been wave after wave of large public protests in cities. Some Iranian residents, such as a large group of Jews, protested by fleeing the country and resettling elsewhere. All of this protest makes sense, since Iran was historically not Muslim, but much older than that—it was the ancient home of Zoroastrianism. It is clear that although authoritarianism persists in Iran, the reaction against it seems to be on the rise.

Provides a good connection back to the previous example

C

Strong detail makes the argument all the more powerful

Authoritarianism comes in many styles and influences various political structures, such as communistic or theocratic ones, around the world. While authoritarianism still exists in both Russia and Iran, each state has experienced its fair share of protests against this form of government. Moreover, democracy has been growing over the last century, spreading across the world. Political systems are malleable, and they may change over the course of many decades or in just a few years. While authoritarianism persists in some countries, resistance to this form of government appears to be spreading faster than the actual style of government. While only time will reveal whether authoritarianism will establish a stronger foothold, it is likely that the current authoritarian governments will be overturned before they spread elsewhere.

Makes a strong connection to the thesis and effectively wraps up the essay's arguments

AP EUROPEAN HISTORY

Short-Answer Questions

Time Limit: 40 minutes

Scoring Range: 0–3 points per question. Each question has three sub-parts (a, b, and c), and each is worth one point.

Description: You'll be asked to analyze, contextualize, and make connections between the provided sources and the historical developments and processes they describe.

- ❑ Question 1 is required, includes 1–2 secondary sources, and focuses on historical developments or processes between the years 1600 and 2001.

- ❑ Question 2 is required, includes 1 primary source, and focuses on historical developments or processes between the years 1600 and 2001.

- ❑ You can choose between Question 3 (which focuses on historical developments or processes between the years 1450 to 1648 and/or the period from 1648 to 1815) and Question 4 (which will involve the years 1815 to 1914 and/or the period from 1914 to present) for the last question. No sources are included for either Question 3 or Question 4.

RUBRIC
How to Earn Points
You'll earn a point for each part of a question that is answered correctly.

Relevant Skills for Short Answer Questions:
- ❯❯ General Advice, **see Chapter 4**
- ❯❯ Short Answer Approaches, **see Chapter 5**
- ❯❯ Analyzing Textual Content, **see Chapter 7**
- ❯❯ Analyzing Quantitative and Graphical Content, **see Chapter 8**

Document-Based Question

Time Limit: 60 minutes, including a 15-minute reading period

Scoring Range: 0–7 points

Description: You'll be presented with seven documents (such as texts, charts, and/or political cartoons) that give various perspectives on a historical development or process. You'll be asked to develop and support an argument based on these documents and other evidence from your own knowledge. The topic of the document-based question will include historical developments or processes between the years 1600 and 2001.

# of Points Available	RUBRIC	
	How to Earn Points	
1	**A**	Respond to the prompt with a historically defensible thesis/claim that establishes a line of reasoning. *The thesis must consist of one or more sentences located in one place, either in the introduction or the conclusion.*
1	**B**	Describe a broader historical context relevant to the prompt, such as historical events, developments, or processes that occur before, during, or continue after the time frame of the question. *This point is not awarded for merely a phrase or reference.*
1	**C**	Use the content of at least three documents. *The response must accurately describe—rather than simply quote—the content from at least three documents, and use the content from the documents to support an argument in response to the prompt.*
1	**D**	Use at least six documents to earn an additional point.
1	**E**	Use at least one additional piece of specific historical evidence (beyond that found in the documents) relevant to an argument about the prompt. *The evidence must be described and must be more than a phrase or reference. This additional piece of evidence must be different from the evidence used to earn the point for contextualization.*

RUBRIC	
# of Points Available	How to Earn Points
1	Explain how or why the document's point of view, purpose, historical situation, and/or audience is relevant to an argument for at least three documents. *The evidence must explain how or why—rather than simply identifying—the document's point of view, purpose, historical situation, or audience is relevant to an argument about the prompt for each of the three documents sourced.*
1	**G** Demonstrate a complex understanding of the historical development that is the focus of the prompt, using evidence to corroborate, qualify, or modify an argument that addresses the question. *This understanding must be part of the argument, not merely a phrase or reference.*

Relevant Skills for Document-Based Question:

- » General Advice, **see Chapter 4**
- » Long Essay Approaches, **see Chapter 6**
- » Analyzing Textual Content, **see Chapter 7**
- » Analyzing Quantitative and Graphical Content, **see Chapter 8**
- » Combining Outside Information and Given Information, **see Chapter 9**
- » Synthesis, **see Chapter 12**
- » Argumentative Essays, **see Chapter 13**

Sample Essay

The prompt for this essay asked about the population policy in fascist Italy and how people reacted to it.

By 1925, Benito Mussolini solidified his power in Italy by creating the Fascist National Party and eliminating all political opposition. In order to strengthen his already powerful regime, Mussolini instituted policies that allied himself and the Fascist Party with Italian conservatives, many of whom were business owners and people of property. The Fascist Party aligned itself with the notion of preserving law and order, and family values. To these ends, Mussolini instituted a decree in 1925 forming the National Organization for the Protection of Mothers and Children. This decree was designed to encourage women to stay home

A

Provides a thesis that responds to the prompt with a clear argument

and have more children, and thus build Italy's population. Although the policy purported to help women and their families, it was doomed to failure, as the Fascists eventually discovered, because while it may be easy for men to legislate and propagandize the female body, the women who were expected to follow these laws suffered greatly, both physically and emotionally.

B — Describes the broader historical context

In the parliamentary decree (Doc. 1), the National Organization for the Protection of Mothers and Children's stated goals were to protect women during pregnancy, assist children of needy parents until the age of five, protect children who were intellectually or physically disabled, abandoned, or delinquent up to the age of 18, provide "helpful" scientific information to help mothers care for the children, and create clinics for prenatal and infant care. While these goals appear quite noble and supportive, what was behind them was the attempt to incentivize women to give up jobs in order to have more children to build up the Italian population. Mussolini, in a speech (Doc. 5), said that work, meaning paid work, makes a woman more "like a man." The danger, he said, was that this will deprive men of their dignity and men will be "castrated in every sense." This language indicates that this decree was not about supporting women but rather about strengthening men. A woman who chose work over a family was "castrating" her husband—preventing the natural process of human evolution and denying men the display of their reproductive fitness, by passing along their strong genes to a new generation of Italians. An article appearing in the Fascist party magazine in honor of Mother and Child Day (Doc. 6) further emphasizes the importance of the woman's role as mother to her (many) children by stressing that this new national holiday was meant to exalt both motherhood and childhood, because, they argued, that without mothers and babies, the nation was "condemned to moral, political, and economic decline." Thus, those who dared to disagree with this population enhancement policy could be accused of being against not only modern, scientific, healthful support of pregnant women and mothers, but also depriving men of their dignity and virility and condemning society to moral, political, and economic decline.

G — Shows a complex understanding of the historical development from the prompt

The women who actually had to bear and raise the children were against these policies. In her memoirs, Mussolini's daughter Edda Mussolini Ciano recalled how angry she was at having been called back to Italy after her husband's diplomat post in China ended (Doc. 7). She described being forced to leave "that spellbinding magical country" only to come home to Italy and wind up pregnant again only two years after the birth of her first child. Ciano also received a letter from another woman asking for help because she was suffering. She identified herself in the letter as the impoverished mother of 11 children, the youngest only a few months old. The woman said the problem was not so much the fact of having the 11 children, but rather that when the husband was called up for military service, the mother found herself unable to care for all these children on her own. She appealed to Mussolini's daughter for a subsidy. This woman had clearly followed Il Duce's decree and wanted the promised financial support. But if she was writing to his daughter, it is likely she did not receive help.

Experts in the social sciences and political refugees saw the folly of the plan as well. A statistics professor (Doc. 3) wrote that his research indicated that economic concerns are directly related to the number of childbirths. He argued that one's economic standing always impacts a family's decision to have children and that the desire for economic stability or even a rise in one's socioeconomic standing would necessarily limit the size of a family. A demographer (Doc. 2) emphasized this point by saying that the sex drive would be limited by one's "preoccupation with survival." A political refugee living in the United States clearly saw that this program in his country of origin was a failure (Doc. 4), and argued that the Fascists also saw this, which made the government push harder to make the policy work. As a result, he said, they increased the propaganda campaign by idealizing the large woman, who weighed 300 pounds or more, as the research indicated that slender women generally had fewer children compared to larger women.

F
Shows how the document is relevant to the argument

C/D
References at least 6 documents in all and uses them to support the thesis

Mussolini's program was doomed to failure. While some women did have larger families, it certainly wasn't enough to make up for the number of Italian soldiers lost in World War II.

E
This essay would not earn the point for this category, as it does not provide additional historical evidence

Long Essay Question

Time Limit: 40 minutes

Scoring Range: 0–6 points

Description: You'll have a choice of three questions; you'll pick one to answer. All test the same skills, but the questions focus primarily on different historical time periods (1450–1700, 1648–1914, or 1815–2001). You'll be asked to develop and support an argument based on evidence.

RUBRIC and SAMPLE ESSAYS
How to Earn Points
See the Long Essay Question information for AP U.S. History, as it is identical other than the region in question.

Relevant Skills for Long Essay Question:

» General Advice, **see Chapter 4**
» Long Essay Approaches, **see Chapter 6**
» Adding Outside Content, **see Chapter 10**
» Argumentative Essays, **see Chapter 13**

AP U.S. HISTORY

Short-Answer Questions

Time Limit: 40 minutes

Scoring Range: 0–3 points per question. Each question has three sub-parts (a, b, and c), and each is worth one point.

Description: You'll be asked to analyze, contextualize, and make connections between the provided sources and the historical developments and processes they describe.

- ❏ Question 1 is required, includes 1–2 secondary sources, and focuses on historical developments or processes between the years 1754 and 1980.

- ❏ Question 2 is required, includes 1 primary source, and focuses on historical developments or processes between the years 1754 and 1980.

- ❏ You can choose between Question 3 (which focuses on historical developments or processes between the years 1491 and 1877) and Question 4 (which focuses on historical developments or processes between the years 1865 and 2001) for the last question. No sources are included for either Question 3 or Question 4.

RUBRIC
How to Earn Points
You'll earn a point for each part of a question that is answered correctly.

Relevant Skills for Short Answer Questions:

- ❯❯ General Advice, **see Chapter 4**
- ❯❯ Short Answer Approaches, **see Chapter 5**
- ❯❯ Analyzing Textual Content, **see Chapter 7**
- ❯❯ Analyzing Quantitative and Graphical Content, **see Chapter 8**

Document-Based Question

Time Limit: 60 minutes (including a 15-minute reading period)

Scoring Range: 0–7 points

Description: You'll be presented with seven documents that give various perspectives on a historical development or process. You'll be asked to develop and support an argument based on these documents and other evidence from your own knowledge. The topic of the document-based question will include historical developments or processes between the years 1754 and 1980.

RUBRIC and SAMPLE ESSAY
How to Earn Points

See the Document-Based Question information for AP European History, as it is identical other than the region in question.

Relevant Skills for Document-Based Question:

- ❯❯ General Advice, **see Chapter 4**
- ❯❯ Long Essay Approaches, **see Chapter 6**
- ❯❯ Analyzing Textual Content, **see Chapter 7**
- ❯❯ Analyzing Quantitative and Graphical Content, **see Chapter 8**
- ❯❯ Combining Outside Information and Given Information, **see Chapter 9**
- ❯❯ Synthesis, **see Chapter 12**
- ❯❯ Argumentative Essays, **see Chapter 13**

Long Essay Question

Time Limit: 40 minutes

Scoring Range: 0–6 points

Description: You'll have a choice of three questions; you'll pick one to answer. Each tests the same skills and reasoning process (e.g., comparison, causation, or continuity and change), but the questions focus on historical developments and processes from different time periods (either the period from 1491 to 1800, from 1800 to 1898, or from 1890 to 2001). You'll be asked to develop and support an argument based on evidence.

RUBRIC		
# of Points Available	**How to Earn Points**	
1	**A**	Respond to the prompt with a historically defensible thesis/claim that establishes a line of reasoning. *The thesis must consist of one or more sentences located in one place, either in the introduction or the conclusion.*
1	**B**	Describe a broader historical context relevant to the prompt, such as historical events, developments, or processes that occur before, during, or continue after the time frame of the question. *This point is not awarded for merely a phrase or reference.*
2	**C**	Support an argument in response to the prompt using specific and relevant examples of historical evidence.
2	**D**	Demonstrate a complex understanding of the historical development that is the focus of the prompt, using evidence to corroborate, qualify, or modify an argument that addresses the question. *This understanding must be part of the argument, not merely a phrase or reference.*

Relevant Skills for Long Essay Question:

» General Advice, **see Chapter 4**
» Long Essay Approaches, **see Chapter 6**
» Adding Outside Content, **see Chapter 10**
» Argumentative Essays, **see Chapter 13**

Sample Essay

The prompt for this essay asked about the extent to which colonial Americans' reaction to British imperial authority in 1754–1776 was influenced by ideas of self-government.

Ideas of self-government greatly influenced American colonial reaction to British imperial authority from 1754 to 1776. For 150 years, the American colonies had mostly been left alone and were quite happy to self-govern. So, when the British came asking for money to pay for the Seven Years' War, it didn't sit right with most of the American colonists who had grown used to the idea that they'd be left to rule as they saw fit. In the end, the American right to self-govern was both about maintaining the way things had been and embracing the new ideas of the Enlightenment, which was about individual freedoms. British taxation and other such acts threatened the autonomy Americans had and threatened the autonomy they thought they deserved.

Perhaps the strongest and most well-known phrase of this time was the idea of "no taxation without representation." Britain had passed acts like the Stamp Act and the Sugar Act to raise money to pay for the war with the French and Native Americans, which was fought to protect the colonies. Americans felt that all the taxes Britain levied to pay for the war were unfair because the Americans had no say in British government. Americans were fine to be left alone as before, but to be taxed with zero benefit was an unwelcome departure from how it had been. This was a threat to the colonial way of life as it had been for a very long time—the American position boiled down to either "let us return to how it was" or "give us representation in Parliament." Anything in between only benefited the British and was met extremely negatively by the colonists.

B Background context sets the stage for the argument and helps the reader understand why this is an issue in the given time period

A Clear thesis statement that follows the previous points

Relates back to thesis statement regarding the past versus new ideas

C Specific historical details support the argument

A specific transition helps with the shift from the last idea to the next

It wasn't just the past way of life that was threatened—the British policies were also inconsistent with the American view of the future. The Enlightenment focused on the idea of "individual freedom." Writers like Thomas Paine in "Common Sense" noted that people should rule themselves and there was no reason to have a King or some ruler who did not need to answer for his actions. This appealed to the colonists greatly: in their view, they had done just fine on their own, and after many generations, most of them had no real allegiance or fondness for the homeland. The sudden re-appearance of Britain in everyday affairs was extremely unwelcome to a people who already felt independent and would only push those people to become more independent. British imperial authority was a threat to the American view of the future—that they could rule themselves more effectively than some King from overseas.

Demonstrates complexity by expanding the argument

The writer follows a similar structure in both body paragraphs: details, analysis, and then support for the thesis

The British imperial policy was a major threat to both how Americans lived before and a view of the future. The taxes passed by Britain showed that America would no longer be left alone but were also inconsistent with the ideas of the Enlightenment that was sweeping the Americas at the time. In a way, we could say that Britain's policies after ignoring the colonists for so long pushed the colonists toward independence that much more quickly and wound up causing another war rather than paying for the first.

The conclusion restates the thesis and the points made, and it ends on a strong statement

AP WORLD HISTORY: MODERN

Short-Answer Questions

Time Limit: 40 minutes

Scoring Range: 0–3 points per question. Each question has three sub-parts (a, b, and c), and each is worth one point.

Description: You'll be asked to analyze, contextualize, and make connections between the provided sources and the historical developments and processes they describe.

- ❏ Question 1 is required, includes 1–2 secondary sources, and focuses on historical developments or processes between the years 1200 and 2001.

- ❏ Question 2 is required, includes 1 primary source, and focuses on historical developments or processes between the years 1200 and 2001.

- ❏ You can choose between Question 3 (which focuses on the period from 1200 to 1750) and Question 4 (which focuses on the period from 1750 to 2001) for the last question. No sources are included for either Question 3 or Question 4.

RUBRIC
How to Earn Points

You'll earn a point for each part of a question that is answered correctly.

Relevant Skills for Short Answer Questions:
- » General Advice, **see Chapter 4**
- » Short Answer Approaches, **see Chapter 5**
- » Analyzing Textual Content, **see Chapter 7**
- » Analyzing Quantitative and Graphical Content, **see Chapter 8**

Document-Based Question

Suggested Time: 60 minutes (including a 15-minute reading period)

Scoring Range: 0–7 points

Description: You'll be presented with seven documents that give various perspectives on a historical development or process. You'll be asked to develop and support an argument based on these documents and other evidence from your own knowledge. The topic of the document-based question will include historical developments or processes between the years 1450 and 2001.

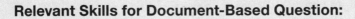

RUBRIC and SAMPLE ESSAY
How to Earn Points

See the Document-Based Question information for AP European History, as it is identical other than the region in question.

Relevant Skills for Document-Based Question:

>> General Advice, **see Chapter 4**

>> Long Essay Approaches, **see Chapter 6**

>> Analyzing Textual Content, **see Chapter 7**

>> Analyzing Quantitative and Graphical Content, **see Chapter 8**

>> Combining Outside Information and Given Information, **see Chapter 9**

>> Synthesis, **see Chapter 12**

>> Argumentative Essays, **see Chapter 13**

Long Essay Question

Suggested Time: 40 minutes (out of 100 minutes total)

Scoring Range: 0–6 points

Description: You'll have a choice of three questions; you'll pick one to answer. Each tests the same skills and reasoning process (e.g., comparison, causation, or continuity and change), but the questions focus on historical developments and processes from different time periods (either the period from 1200 to 1750, from 1450 to 1900, or from 1750 to 2001). You'll be asked to develop and support an argument based on evidence.

RUBRIC and SAMPLE ESSAY
How to Earn Points
See the Long Essay Question information for AP U.S. History, as it is identical other than the region in question.

Relevant Skills for Long Essay Question:

>> General Advice, **see Chapter 4**
>> Long Essay Approaches, **see Chapter 6**
>> Adding Outside Content, **see Chapter 10**
>> Argumentative Essays, **see Chapter 13**

AP U.S. GOVERNMENT AND POLITICS

Questions 1–3: Short Answer

 Suggested Time: 20 minutes each (out of 100 minutes total)

 Scoring Range: 0–3 or 0–4 points each

Description:

❑ One Concept Application will ask you to describe and explain the effects of a political institution, behavior, or process and transfer understanding of course concepts to apply them in a new situation or scenario.

❑ One Quantitative Analysis will provide quantitative information (a graph, map, table, or infographic) and ask you to describe the data, connect it to political principles, and draw a conclusion.

❑ One SCOTUS Comparison will ask you to analyze a non-required Supreme Court Case and its holding and compare it to a specified Supreme Court Case required in the course.

RUBRIC
How to Earn Points
The prompt will provide 3–4 tasks for each short-answer question. You'll earn a point for each task that is completed correctly.

Relevant Skills for Short Answer Question:

» General Advice, **see Chapter 4**
» Short Answer Approaches, **see Chapter 5**
» Analyzing Textual Content, **see Chapter 7**
» Analyzing Quantitative and Graphical Content, **see Chapter 8**

Argument Essay

Suggested Time: 40 minutes (out of 100 minutes total)

Scoring Range: 0–6 points

Description: You'll write an evidence-based essay supporting a claim or thesis involving course concepts and foundational documents.

# of Points Available		How to Earn Points
	RUBRIC	
1	**A**	Respond to the prompt with a defensible claim or thesis that establishes a line of reasoning. *The thesis can be located anywhere in the response.*
3	**B**	Use two pieces of specific and relevant evidence to support the claim or thesis. *To earn all three points, you must use one of the foundational documents listed in the prompt.*
1	**C**	Explain how or why the evidence supports the claim or thesis.
1	**D**	Respond to an opposing or alternate perspective using refutation, concession, or rebuttal.

Relevant Skills for Argument Essay:

» General Advice, **see Chapter 4**
» Long Essay Approaches, **see Chapter 6**
» Adding Outside Content, **see Chapter 10**
» Argumentative Essays, **see Chapter 13**

Sample Essay

The prompt for this essay asked whether a strong Executive branch is the best way of ensuring a republican form of government's long-term survival and instructed students to use evidence from foundational documents used in the AP course and to respond to an opposing point of view.

Within the United States' federal government, power is shared by three distinct branches: the Executive, Legislative, and Judicial. In theory, the three branches should share power equally with each other and also serve as checks on each other's power. The Executive branch has powers that the Legislative and Judicial do not, and vice versa. However, at times in U.S. history, one branch may have had more power than the others. Some may claim that we live in the age of strong Executive power with Executive orders and military actions bypassing the approval of Congress. If this is true, the expanding power of the Executive branch benefits the long-term survival of a republican form of government because it prevents the inevitable delays inherent in a government dominated by the Legislative and Judicial branches.

Under the United States' first foundational document, the Articles of Confederation, there WAS no Executive branch to speak of. There was no President of the United States. Because of this, the Articles of Confederation were very weak, and were unable to be administered or enforced effectively. One of the weakest points of the Articles was the inability for the federal government to raise taxes. Thus, the federal government was unable to afford an army. Famously, the federal government was unable to suppress Shay's Rebellion. The Articles of Confederation give us strong reason to suggest that a strong Executive branch is beneficial, because the lack of one led to at least one rebellion that was unable to be put down due to a weak federal government and ineffective leadership overall. When the Articles were replaced by the Constitution and President George Washington was given adequate power, he was able to suppress the Whiskey Rebellion only a few years later.

The benefit of a strong Executive branch is also found in Alexander Hamilton's Federalist No. 70. Hamilton argues that the Executive branch can act quickly and decisively, but also has great accountability to the people. Throughout Federalist No. 70, Hamilton refers to the "energy" found only in the Executive: because the Executive branch is run by one person, it provides unity of purpose. Unlike the inevitable disagreements that happen in the Legislative and Judicial branches, a President can surround him/herself with like-minded people—or fire them if they do not comply.

Provides background information before introducing the thesis statement

A
Articulates a defensible thesis that responds to the prompt and establishes a line of reasoning

C
Explains how or why the evidence supports the thesis

B
References multiple foundational documents

References
and refutes
an alternative
viewpoint

Although some people may claim that expanding the powers of the Executive branch is harmful, as stated in Brutus No. 1, Hamilton pointed out that the Executive branch is also the most accountable to the people. It is easier to point the blame at one person, the President, than it is to blame the entire Congress or members of the Supreme Court. According to Hamilton, this would provide a good incentive toward good behavior and judgment. Hamilton even goes so far as to claim that divisions between leaders, as can happen in Congress, are more dangerous to the long-term health of a republic.

Within the federal government, there exist several forms of checks and balances and separation of powers, as Federalist No. 51 points out. These separations of powers prevent many of our fears, such as the President becoming too much like a king. With the powers of Congress and the Judicial branch, these issues can be resolved quickly. The fear of a tyrannical Executive that would lord it over the other branches is an unrealistic one built on ignorance of the government's structure. Because of these systems currently in place, the Executive branch can wield power while at the same time not infringing on the powers granted to the other branches.

Conclusion restates
the thesis, recalls the
evidence used in the
body paragraphs, and
ends with a concluding
thought

Chapter 2

Language AP Exams

AP CHINESE LANGUAGE AND CULTURE

Question 1: Story Narration

Suggested Time: 15 minutes each (out of 30 minutes total)

Scoring Range: Scored holistically from 0–6 points

Description: You will be asked to narrate a story suggested by a series of pictures.

RUBRIC	
Scored based on how well you...	• Include a beginning, middle, and end • Tell a story consistent with the images • Organize your story and use transitions • Use correct and appropriate grammar, vocabulary, and register
Description of an essay scoring 4:	These essays tell a complete story consistent with the stimulus but may lack detail or elaboration or have minor inconsistencies in their logical progression from beginning to end. They are generally organized and coherent; use of transitional elements and cohesive devices may be inconsistent; discourse of paragraph length, although sentences may be loosely connected. They may include several lapses in otherwise consistent use of register appropriate to situation, mostly appropriate vocabulary, and idioms with errors that do not generally obscure meaning. They include mostly appropriate grammatical structures, with errors that do not generally obscure meaning.

To earn a 5 or a 6, add more detail and use more sophisticated vocabulary and grammatical structures.

Relevant Skills for Story Narration:

》 General Advice, **see Chapter 4**

》 Analyzing Quantitative and Graphical Content, **see Chapter 8**

》 Foreign Language Essays, **see Chapter 15**

Question 2: Email Reply

Suggested Time: 15 minutes each (out of 30 minutes total)

Scoring Range: Scored holistically from 0–6 points

Description: You will be asked to read and answer an email message.

RUBRIC	
Scored based on how well you...	• Address all aspects of the prompt and respond to all questions in the original email • Organize your email effectively and use transitions • Use correct and appropriate grammar, vocabulary, and register
Description of an essay scoring 4:	These essays address all aspects of the stimulus but may lack detail or elaboration. They are generally organized and coherent; use of transitional elements and cohesive devices may be inconsistent; discourse of paragraph length, although sentences may be loosely connected. They may include several lapses in otherwise consistent use of register appropriate to situation, mostly appropriate vocabulary, and idioms with errors that do not generally obscure meaning. They include mostly appropriate grammatical structures, with errors that do not generally obscure meaning.

To earn a 5 or a 6, add more detail and use more sophisticated vocabulary and grammatical structures.

Relevant Skills for Email Reply:

>> General Advice, **see Chapter 4**
>> Foreign Language Essays, **see Chapter 15**
>> Email Reply Writing, **see Chapter 16**

Sample Essay

See the chapter on Email Reply Writing for specific advice and examples.

AP ENGLISH LANGUAGE AND COMPOSITION

Question 1: Synthesis Essay

Suggested Time: 40 minutes (out of 135 minutes total, including a 15-minute reading period)

Scoring Range: 0–6 points

Description: After reading 6–7 texts about a topic (including visual and quantitative sources), you will be asked to compose an argument that combines and cites at least 3 of the sources to support your thesis.

# of Points Available		How to Earn Points
		RUBRIC
1	**A**	Respond to the prompt with a thesis that presents a defensible position. *The thesis may be one or more sentences, anywhere in the essay.*
4	**B**	Provide specific evidence from at least three of the provided sources to support all claims in a line of reasoning and consistently explain how the evidence supports a line of reasoning. *You cannot earn all 4 points if your writing has grammar and/or mechanical errors that interfere with communication.*
1	**C**	Demonstrate sophistication of thought and/or a complex understanding of the rhetorical situation. *This point is based on the argument as a whole, not a single phrase or reference.*
1	**D**	Respond to an opposing or alternate perspective using refutation, concession, or rebuttal.

Relevant Skills for Synthesis Essay:

» General Advice, **see Chapter 4**

» Long Essay Approaches, **see Chapter 6**

» Analyzing Textual Content, **see Chapter 7**

» Analyzing Quantitative and Graphical Content, **see Chapter 8**

» Combining Outside Information and Given Information, **see Chapter 9**

» Synthesis, **see Chapter 12**

» Argumentative Essays, **see Chapter 13**

Sample Essay

The prompt for this essay asked whether gift giving should be embraced or feared and provided seven sources with different perspectives on the issue.

A

Responds to the prompt with a clear position

Like a sunset or an inside joke, gift giving is meant to be embraced. Gift giving can spark genuine joy and facilitate human connection. Its presence in other species lends credit to the idea that gift giving has evolved as a practice that reinforces the social contract. For these reasons and more, gift giving is absolutely worth the cost.

A

Outlines arguments that support the position

B

Uses at least 3 sources

Many dread gift shopping, but the experience doesn't have to be a joyless bother. Source B illustrates a most peculiar phenomenon: a pet cat who keeps presenting stolen swimming goggles to her owner. While we may never know what exactly motivated the cat to gift its owner with swimming goggles, the "celebrity" of the gifting kitty illustrates the simple joy that gift giving can bring even to people who did not give or receive the gift. Likewise, the poem in Source A is a series of instructions for how to give both effectively and whole-heartedly. Taken together, these instructions paint an ideal picture of gift giving: a loving experience performed "from the heart" as well as with utmost care and thoughtfulness to what is needed. How could the act of giving or receiving such a gift fail to be a joyful experience? Clearly, gift giving can be a joyous addition to one's life.

Clearly explains examples and indicates how they contribute to the arguments

Relates the argument back to the author's position

Gift giving can also facilitate human connection. During quarantine, my aunt Lisa and I cannot travel to see each other, so we have exchanged several small gifts throughout the year: T-shirts, hats, crafting supplies, etc. This running exchange has helped me feel closer to her in spite of the distance between us. Those who call for "no-gift holidays" like in Source D must acknowledge that with the growth of online shopping and a renaissance of the crafting arts, gift giving isn't necessarily a "nightmare of consumerism" for everyone. Instead, one could opt for "a loving message in a card, a date for a cup of coffee and conversation, an afternoon of chores" (Source D). Gifting experiences is a valid way to express one's affections. For example, my dad taught me how to drive. He gave me the gifts of his time and expertise. In fact, his giving fits every line of "The Gift of Giving" poem (Source A), which makes me appreciate it all the more. His gift to me came without obligation or a burdensome expectation of "reciprocity" (Source E). For me, gift giving has always been one of many ways to connect with family. Now, gift giving has given us a way to keep connecting despite current challenges.

Gift giving not only can but invariably does reinforce roles and relationships. According to Source E, "there's no such thing as a gift in a vacuum," and we are inherently influenced by "the whole cultural thing." Crows have been found to bring "gifts" of brightly colored trash to other crows and humans alike. Dolphins, too, have been spotted presenting each other with "gifts" of colorful rocks in a form of courtship. Taken together, these examples of how crows, dolphins, and even cats (Source B) display gift-giving behavior further support the idea that gift giving is an important behavior for us as social creatures. Understandably, then, gift giving has a long human history, with "many different meanings cross-culturally" (Source E). Gifts have been expected as a "sign of hospitality" from "pre-modern Japan" to present-day Mexico (Source E), perhaps helping to ensure that weary travelers had their needs met. On the other hand, my family has always followed a tradition of bringing gifts for ones' hosts, possibly to show our appreciation of all that goes into hosting visiting relatives. Regardless of the specific scenario, the tradition of gift giving is irrevocably linked with how we relate to each other.

For those who, like the eponymous Grinch, detest the gift-giving traditions that inevitably accompany major holidays and milestones, consider this: while both gift givers and gift receivers report increased feelings of happiness after a gifting, the givers reported more, longer lasting happiness (Source C). The gift giver may bear the burdens of time and expense, but he or she can be rewarded with a feeling of joy, a chance to connect with someone important to him or her, or even the understanding that we are all more interconnected than we think. In a world where people are cut off from each other and from their lives before quarantine, gift giving can connect us to each other and remind us of our shared histories. Hopefully, we make use of what a gift that is.

Question 2: Rhetorical Analysis Essay

Suggested Time: 40 minutes (out of 135 minutes total, including a 15-minute reading period)

Scoring Range: 0–6 points

Description: After reading a nonfiction text, you will be asked to analyze how the writer's language choices contribute to the intended meaning and purpose of the text.

RUBRIC	
# of Points Available	**How to Earn Points**
1	**A** Respond to the prompt with a defensible thesis that analyzes the writer's rhetorical choices. *The thesis may be one or more sentences, anywhere in the essay.*
4	**B** Provide specific evidence to support all claims in a line of reasoning, consistently explain how the evidence supports a line of reasoning, and explain how multiple rhetorical choices in the passage contribute to the writer's argument, purpose, or message. *You cannot earn all 4 points if your writing has grammar and/or mechanical errors that interfere with communication. To earn the fourth point, the response may observe multiple instances of the same rhetorical choice if each instance further contributes to the argument, purpose, or message of the passage.*
1	**C** Demonstrate sophistication of thought and/or a complex understanding of the rhetorical situation. *This point is based on the argument as a whole, not a single phrase or reference.*

Relevant Skills for Rhetorical Analysis Essay:

» General Advice, **see Chapter 4**

» Long Essay Approaches, **see Chapter 6**

» Rhetorical Analysis, **see Chapter 11**

Sample Essay

The prompt for this essay provided a letter from Abraham Lincoln and asked students to analyze Lincoln's rhetorical strategies in persuading his audience that he could not end slavery at that time.

While Abraham Lincoln is known today for freeing the slaves with his Emancipation Proclamation, those who lived through such times did not have the luxury of historical perspective. Who can know how many people died waiting for freedom? How many people in this country were poisoned by the practice of slavery before it was outlawed in practice? Shortly before he freed the slaves, Lincoln was advancing an argument about timing, replying to a request for a Proclamation of Emancipation with the argument that he should not yet issue one. In his letter, Lincoln appeals to trusting one's creator, being rationally-minded, and validating the audience in pursuit of patience on issuing a proclamation.

Lincoln makes multiple appeals to a God shared by him and his audience in order to assert his position. In the first paragraph, he claims that his role as the president ensures God would speak to him, if such were possible: "it might be supposed [God] would reveal [his will] directly to me." Moreover, he intends to follow the will of God as closely as possible: "if I can learn what [God's will] is I will do it!" Here, Lincoln is calling upon his audience's trust in its creator to validate his message. This must represent a significant persuasive strategy for Lincoln, as he calls back to the idea in the last paragraph: "whatever shall appear to be God's will, I will do." Clearly, Lincoln expects such language to build his audience's trust in him. His appeals to God add credibility to both him as a person and the idea that the proclamation is in his hands alone.

Lincoln also appeals to logos, building his argument with cool logic. In the first paragraph, he follows a discussion of God's will in the matter with a caution that he will still "study the plain physical facts of the case, ascertain what is possible, and learn what appears to be wise and right" before a proclamation, all of which is a very practical example of common sense and wisdom. Carefully, so as not to suggest that the two qualities are in any way opposed, Lincoln assures his audience that any decision on his proclamation will be not only divine but also logical. In the third paragraph, Lincoln asks how the nation can "feed and care for such a multitude" of freed slaves. He returns to the demographics argument in the fifth paragraph, insinuating that a proclamation would potentially alienate "fifty thousand bayonets in the Union armies from the border slave States." Even Lincoln, the president of the embattled United States, was at the mercy of "possible consequences of insurrection and massacre" on the part of the South should he issue the proclamation. For Lincoln, issuing a proclamation is a "practical war measure." Essentially, Lincoln reduced the proclamation to being not

---

A Clearly states the thesis and outlines the rhetorical choices that will be discussed

B Identifies the same strategy in multiple points of the text

Rhetorical questions show command of language

Follows the outline of rhetorical choices from the introduction

B Explains how the evidence supports a line of reasoning

only ineffective but also potentially very deadly, further evidencing the idea that logically, only he, "commander-in-chief of the army and navy," can decide when—or if—to issue a proclamation.

Lincoln further enhances both his credibility and position by validating arguments for immediately producing a proclamation for audience demand. In the fifth paragraph, Lincoln yields that "slavery is the root of the rebellion" and that "emancipation would help [the U.S.] in Europe" and "weaken the rebels by drawing off their laborers" at home, all of which point toward immediately issuing a Proclamation of Emancipation as his audience demands. Lincoln, however, clarifies that the loyalty of "fifty thousand bayonets in the Union armies from the border slave States" separates him from a proclamation, effectively countering the military advantage of issuing a proclamation. Lincoln defends his position by weakening arguments for him to act immediately. "The subject," he says, "is on my mind, by day and night, more than any other." Lincoln yet again assures his letter's audience that while their concerns are valid, he is more than capable of handling the gravity of the proclamation himself.

Through appeals to trusting one's creator, being rationally-minded, and validating the audience, Lincoln offers his audience a persuasive message: only he is qualified to make the best decision about issuing a proclamation against slavery. History will never know what could have been different had Lincoln waited longer—or even indefinitely—to make the Emancipation Proclamation. But more importantly, can students of history learn to do the right thing more quickly than their forebears did? Can today's Americans celebrate the figure of Abraham Lincoln and still aspire to surpass him in some respects? Indeed, for what it reveals about everyone, Lincoln's reply all those years ago might be just as relevant today.

> Good use of embedded quotes to further the argument with specific evidence

> **B**
> Explains how the writer's use of rhetorical choices contributes to this interpretation of passage

> Ends with a concluding thought. Does not necessarily earn the sophistication point, as the essay does not examine complexities in an above-and-beyond manner.

Question 3: Argument Essay

Suggested Time: 40 minutes (out of 135 minutes total, including a 15-minute reading period)

Scoring Range: 0–6 points

Description: This long essay will ask you to create an evidence-based argument that responds to a given topic.

RUBRIC	
# of Points Available	**How to Earn Points**
1	**A** Respond to the prompt with a thesis that presents a defensible position. *The thesis may be one or more sentences, anywhere in the essay.*
4	**B** Provide specific evidence to support all claims in a line of reasoning and consistently explain how the evidence supports a line of reasoning. *You cannot earn all 4 points if your writing has grammar and/or mechanical errors that interfere with communication.*
1	**C** Demonstrate sophistication of thought and/or a complex understanding of the rhetorical situation. *This point is based on the argument as a whole, not a single phrase or reference.*

Relevant Skills for Argument Essay:

» General Advice, **see Chapter 4**
» Long Essay Approaches, **see Chapter 6**
» Adding Outside Content, **see Chapter 10**
» Argumentative Essays, **see Chapter 13**

Sample Essay

This prompt asked students to choose something they feel is "overrated" and explain how and why through reasoning and examples.

Ever since I can remember, I've wondered if I will ever get married or find one person to spend my life with. Growing up, I buried my nose in romances such as <u>Sense and Sensibility</u> and fawned over fictional couples like Gomez and Morticia Addams. I envied people like my parents, who seemed to have found their best friend in each other. For all that, should I find my person, a lavish wedding ceremony won't be on the agenda. Wedding culture dictates that couples spend massive amounts of money, reinforces archaic, sexist traditions, and isn't a necessary part of happily ever after. Love is grand, but big weddings are, in a word, overrated.

Weddings, which typically last half a day, can be as expensive as buying and keeping a car, or even a house. My neighbor's wedding reportedly cost $80,000, which is the same price as 4 years of in-state tuition at my first choice university. I can't help but imagine what else the couple could have done with $80,000 besides having a party: put a down payment on a house, started college funds for future kids, or perhaps done some good in the wider community. During COVID, I have read about multiple couples who donated food and catering services from their canceled weddings to unhoused people. One Turkish couple who did have a spectacular wedding replaced their traditional wedding banquet feast with food for thousands of Syrian refugees. Even without spreading their wealth around, couples who spend lots of money on weddings are missing out on opportunities to invest in themselves. What better way to celebrate one's marriage than by putting aside money to have a honeymoon every year or a cabin to retreat to together? Spending tens or even hundreds of thousands of dollars on a single party is grossly overrated.

Wedding culture shows how women were (and still are) treated very differently. The white dress that a bride wears signifies how her value lies in her purity and not in her person. The act of a father walking a bride down the aisle represents how he passes his ownership of her to her husband. Women like my mother and grandmother had to promise to obey their husbands, while their husbands made no such promise in return. Even permission to marry has often been asked of the bride's father rather than the bride herself. These tiresome, outdated rituals are a pitfall of every big wedding I have attended, proving that in my experience, wedding culture has yet to divorce itself from patriarchy. For being stuck in the past, wedding culture is overrated.

A

Outlines arguments that support the position

B

Uses examples from observations to support the argument

A

Responds to the prompt with a clear position

B

Uses examples from personal experience to support the argument

Reinforces the position

According to multiple reality TV shows, lavish weddings do not correlate to enriched relationships. Bridezillas portrays brides who become demanding and even lose touch with reality in pursuit of throwing elaborate dream weddings. On Say Yes to the Dress, brides travel from all over the country to buy wedding dresses from one particular store. Imagine how much more rewarding their lives could be if these brides invested that effort and energy into their relationships, families, or careers. While a Kardashian publicly televised her multimillion dollar first wedding, which tragically ended in divorce, my cousin eloped, marrying her husband in blue jeans, and she's been happily married for a decade. Clearly, how a couple celebrates its commitment has nothing to do with either the strength or duration of that commitment. Big weddings are an overrated part of marriage.

For the crimes of being expensive, misogynistic, and superfluous, wedding culture is nothing if not overrated. Overrated, however, is not inexcusable. This exercise has led me to consider what I would do if my person were to want a lavish wedding. Big weddings are expensive, but making a loved one happy is truly priceless.

> **B** Uses examples from popular culture to support argument; a higher-scoring essay might use more academic examples

> Reiterates arguments and position

> Demonstrates further implications/broader context of the position. Does not necessarily earn a point for sophistication, as the argument is not complex.

AP ENGLISH LITERATURE AND COMPOSITION

Question 1: Poetry Analysis Long Essay

Suggested Time: 40 minutes (out of 120 minutes total)

Scoring Range: 0–6 points

Description: After reading a passage of poetry, you will be asked to respond to the prompt with a thesis that presents a poetic interpretation backed up by evidence.

RUBRIC	
# of Points Available	**How to Earn Points**
1 **A**	Respond to the prompt with a thesis that presents a defensive interpretation of the selected work. *The thesis may be one or more sentences, anywhere in the essay.*
4 **B**	Provide specific evidence to support all claims in a line of reasoning, consistently explain how the evidence supports a line of reasoning, and explain how multiple literary elements or techniques in the poem contribute to its meaning. *You cannot earn all 4 points if your writing has grammar and/or mechanical errors that interfere with communication. To earn the fourth point, the response may observe multiple instances of the same literary element or technique if each instance further contributes to the meaning of the poem.*
1 **C**	Demonstrate sophistication of thought and/or develop a complex literary argument. *This point is based on the argument as a whole, not a single phrase or reference.*

> ## Relevant Skills for Poetry Analysis Long Essay:
>
> » General Advice, **see Chapter 4**
> » Long Essay Approaches, **see Chapter 6**
> » Rhetorical Analysis, **see Chapter 11**

Sample Essay

The prompt for this essay provided a poem and asked students to analyze how the author's literary techniques develop the complex meanings attributed to the quilt in the poem.

Marilyn Nelson Waniek's poem "The Century Quilt" expresses the speaker's deep emotional attachment to her treasured quilt and the significance that she attributes to it in connecting with her past and present. Waniek explores the themes of family, heritage, and dreams of the future through a variety of literary techniques such as vivid imagery, a free but deliberate structure, and a reflective tone.

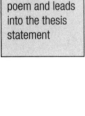

A

Provides a brief summary of the poem and leads into the thesis statement

Previews the techniques that will be discussed in the body paragraphs

The poem employs extensive imagery to build the speaker's world. The use of color is especially significant and carries deep connotations beyond the visual picture that it paints for the reader. The poem opens with a flashback to the speaker's childhood: "My sister and I were in love/with Meema's Indian blanket. We fell asleep under army green/ issued to Daddy by Supply." "Army green" clearly comes across as plain and utilitarian; one can almost feel the scratchiness of the standard-issue military blanket the girls sleep under. Meema's Indian blanket, meanwhile, would be patterned and vibrant, not to mention strongly linked in memory to its owner, the speaker's beloved grandmother. As an adult, she finds the perfect quilt and describes it in terms of its neutral, soothing colors and pattern: "Six Van Dyke brown squares,/two white ones, and one square/the yellowbrown of Mama's cheeks." While this is a literal description, at this point there is a shift in the meaning that color carries throughout the rest of the poem. At this point, it becomes a clear signifier of race and alludes to the complex attitudes contained within the speaker's multiethnic background. She imagines her Meema growing up in Kentucky, "among her yellow sisters,/their grandfather's white family/nodding at them when they met." The cordial reception these white relatives give the evidently mixed-race sisters is very evocative of the emotional and physical distance between them and the tension that would have underlay their meeting in an era when racism was commonplace. She goes on to imagine her potential dreams

C

Identifying opposition shows understanding of complexity

B

Makes the connection between what the author does and its poetic effect

under the quilt, including recollections of her childhood and her father's "burnt umber pride" and mother's "ochre gentleness." The use of color to describe these personality traits reflects the importance of the speaker's heritage to her. In addition, the speaker paints vivid pictures of family activities, such as her and her sister playing pretend while wrapped in Meema's Indian blanket and later her imagined portrait of Meema and her sisters as girls, dancing around to the sounds of their pianola. Combined, these multiple, eloquent uses of imagery clearly express the link that the speaker forms between her quilt and her racial and family identity.

Concludes the paragraph with a sentence that ties the ideas together and circles back to the thesis

In more subtle ways, the structure of "The Century Quilt" also helps express the importance of the quilt to the speaker. The poem is written in free verse and would appear not to have any particular pattern to it, but the line breaks are deliberately placed to create a relaxed, conversational quality. The lack of meter and rhyme scheme allows Waniek to mimic the natural speech patterns that she might use when telling the story. In the first stanza, she says, "When Meema came to live with us/she brought her medicines, her cane,/and the blanket I found on my sister's bed/the last time I visited her." The line breaks in this section occur in places where the speaker would naturally pause. This occurs in other places as well, especially when the speaker is listing things, such as near the end: "Perhaps under this quilt/I'd dream of myself,/of my childhood of miracles/of my father's burnt umber pride/my mother's ochre gentleness." Again, the pauses after the introductory phrase and after each item in her list of dreams feel extremely natural. The effect of placing line breaks to follow a speaking cadence create an intimate, narrative mood, as if the audience is gathered around a fire with the speaker, listening to her tell the story of her quilt.

Transitions improve the flow of the essay

B

Analyzes another feature of the poem and states its effect

In addition to the ways in which the structure contributes to the overall feel of the poem, Waniek uses a reflective, peaceful tone to convey the speaker's deep love for the quilt. "The Century Quilt" compels her to reminisce about the Indian blanket of her childhood and her Meema's childhood. She speaks of that blanket with deep affection, saying that she and her sister "were in love" with it and fondly remembering "how we used to wrap ourselves/at play in its folds and be chieftains/and princesses." Although her sister inherited the treasured Indian blanket instead of her, she finds its replacement: "a quilt/I'd like to die under." The way that she speaks of the quilt suggests that it brings her all of the childhood comfort that she drew from Meema's blanket. The image of the leaves stitched into its squares "whose fingers I imagine/would caress me into the silence" conjures a sense of being peacefully wrapped in its comfort until she passes from this life. That feeling of tranquility continues into the third stanza as she believes she would "have good dreams/for a hundred years under this quilt" and quietly

Basic but effective transition and topic sentence

meditates on both what those dreams might look like and what she imagines her Meema must have dreamed under her Indian blanket. Those dreams are all about family: she imagines Meema "must have dreamed about Mama," her daughter and the speaker's mother, "a lanky girl trailing after her father." The speaker supposes that she would dream of her own past and future, of her parents' love and her "child-hood of miracles," as well as meeting her own "as yet unconceived" child—just as her grandmother would have envisioned her mother. The importance of family to the speaker is paramount, and she speaks of her ancestors with a sense of pride. The repeated references to being "under the quilt" and dreaming transport the reader to a place of warm comfort and contemplation.

Through the use of strong imagery (particularly the deeply layered meanings expressed through color), deliberate choices in structuring the poem's free verse, and the reflective tone, Marilyn Nelson Wan-iek conveys the deeply rooted attachment to her family, heritage, and future that the speaker attributes to her treasured quilt. While she may not have the beloved family heirloom of her childhood, she has found its equal in "The Century Quilt."

> Restates the thesis and recaps the examples in the conclusion

> A thoughtful concluding sentence brings the essay to a strong ending

Question 2: Prose Fiction Analysis Long Essay

Suggested Time: 40 minutes (out of 120 minutes total)

Scoring Range: 0–6 points

Description: After reading a passage of prose fiction (which may include drama), you will be asked to respond to the prompt with a thesis that presents a literary interpretation backed up by evidence.

RUBRIC
How to Earn Points
See the rubric from Question 1—Poetry Analysis Long Essay, as the two rubrics are identical.

Relevant Skills for Prose Fiction Analysis Long Essay:

» General Advice, **see Chapter 4**
» Long Essay Approaches, **see Chapter 6**
» Rhetorical Analysis, **see Chapter 11**

Sample Essay

The prompt for this essay provided an excerpt from a novel and asked students to analyze how the author's use of literary devices characterizes the woman and her situation.

In his novel <u>The Rainbow</u>, D.H. Lawrence characterizes the woman at the center of the Brangwen clan, a family of English farmers, as someone thirsty for knowledge and yearning for a world beyond her own. From the confines of the farm, she gazes "outwards" toward distant cities, envisioning the men there who "were set out to discover what was beyond, to enlarge their own scope and range and freedom." This lies in sharp contrast to the "inwards" facing Brangwen men who surround her, occupied and fulfilled by the strenuous, earthbound work of the farm.

Lawrence uses strong imagery, repetition, and a variety of similes and metaphors to draw the contrast between the simple world the woman knows and the one that she longs for, one with the promise of freedom, knowledge, and power.

A

Opening sentences provide a brief summary of the passage, lay out the thesis, and preview the devices that will be discussed

The passage opens with a vivid description of the intense manual labor the men perform and the satisfaction they draw from it. Lawrence utilizes evocative imagery to paint a picture of them at work: "the earth heaved and opened its furrow to them, [...] the wind blew to dry the wet wheat, and set the young ears of corn wheeling freshly round about." The reader can visualize the open fields, the warm sun, and the dark, freshly turned soil. The men feel "full and surcharged," drawing a sense of gratification and power from their toils. However, Lawrence also paints them as single-minded in their pursuit: "their faces always turned to the heat of the blood, staring into the sun, dazed [...], unable to turn around." Their work of "creation" is their reason for being—it never occurs to them to want more. This is immediately juxtaposed against the woman longing for a different life altogether, one not of "blood-intimacy." Here again, Lawrence uses deliberate word choices to show the outside world through the woman's eyes. The description of distant cities as "the magic land to her, where secrets were made known and desires fulfilled" convey her sense of wonderment and longing for a life driven by knowledge, creativity, and freedom. To her, the world of the learned, creative man is mysterious and alluring. As the woman's thoughts turn in the fourth paragraph to the local vicar, she views him with a sort of mystical quality, once again using the term "magic" to describe his language and contrasting his "other, finer bearing" with that of her husband and the other men around her, who are portrayed as earthy and strong, but slow and dull. The vicar's refinement and intelligence imbue him with a certain power and elevated status that the woman yearns to not just understand, but share. As she ponders what propels this man to a state of higher being, she decides that the answer must be his learnedness, and she longs to achieve this same sort of status.

B

Embedded quotes provide evidence to support the claims

C

Identifies opposition in the text, which shows understanding of complexity

B

Examples are explained and analyzed, not just mentioned

Topic sentences make the organization clear

At several points in the passage, Lawrence uses repetition to accomplish a variety of effects. In the opening sentence, the phrase "it was enough" is repeated to convey the satisfaction that the men draw from their labor, while simultaneously foreshadowing that the woman does not feel the same. Lawrence also describes their environment as "warmth and generating and pain and death" found in their "blood, earth and sky and beast and green plants"; the repeated conjunction "and" in these lists reinforces the repetitive nature of their lives as they do the same work day in, day out. The callback to this device in the third paragraph works to convey the woman's restlessness and boredom with her mundane life, contrasting her husband's constant return to "sky and harvest and beast and land" with her desire to know the outside world. Lawrence employs repetition to a different effect in the final paragraph, throughout a series of rhetorical questions showing the woman's determination in trying to understand what gives the vicar his superior demeanor. She repeatedly asks "what was it" about him that elevated him above men like her husband. Lawrence also repeats the word "craved"—"She craved to know. She craved to achieve this higher being..."—to emphasize the burning curiosity and desire for clarity that this woman feels. She needs a taste of this outside world. This near-desperation is once again demonstrated through the repetition in her final question: "And why—why?" Whereas earlier in the passage, repetition is used to echo the repetitive nature of life on the farm that the woman fights against, in the final paragraph it outlines the woman's thought process in trying to analyze the vicar's demeanor and the depth of her desire to grasp it for herself.

> Neatly wraps up the paragraph with a conclud-ing sentence that ties all of the ideas together and calls back to the thesis

Finally, several metaphors and similes are used to express the woman's worldview. Lawrence repeatedly refers to the men's work on the farm in terms such as "the heat of the blood" and "the pulsing heat of creation" to convey its visceral, brutish nature. The woman sees this as the base state of man and imagines the journey to the life of knowledge and exploration as a battle to break free from it. To speak of moving within this world as a "conquest" and a fight "being waged on the edge of the unknown" is to show the reverence that the wom-an feels for those who have achieved it. She longs to be one of them and views herself as a would-be fighter. Her regard (or lack thereof) for her husband comes through in the final paragraph when she likens the vicar's dominion over him to the power that he himself holds over his cattle. The simile drawn between her husband, or the common man in general, and a bull establishes a clear picture of him as strong in body but weak in mind when compared to the much smaller vicar. Addition-ally, it puts the power dynamic between the two men in terms that a farm wife would likely think in, as she would see every day that "any man is little and frail beside a bull, and yet stronger." By placing the contrast into a familiar context, she is able to determine that the key difference between her husband and the vicar, just as it is between beast and man, is knowledge.

> Good use of vocabu-lary to add sophistication

> Adds context to show broader understanding of the text's themes

> Recaps the thesis in the conclusion

In this brief passage, the woman is vividly depicted as someone who aspires to a life greater than her own. Through the use of detailed imagery, deliberate repetition, and comparisons, we are allowed to view the world through the eyes of someone confined by her circumstances who longs to explore and conquer the unknown.

> Recaps the examples

> Ends with a concluding thought

Question 3: Literary Argument Long Essay

Suggested Time: 40 minutes (out of 120 minutes total)

Scoring Range: 0–6 points

Description: This long essay will ask you to analyze how a literary concept or idea contributes to an interpretation of a literary work, based on a list of provided works or a work from your own reading, and to create an evidence-based argument.

RUBRIC	
# of Points Available	**How to Earn Points**
1	**A** Respond to the prompt with a thesis that presents a defensive interpretation of the selected work. *The thesis may be one or more sentences, anywhere in the essay.*
4	**B** Provide specific evidence to support all claims in a line of reasoning and consistently explain how the evidence supports a line of reasoning. *You cannot earn all 4 points if your writing has grammar and/or mechanical errors that interfere with communication. To earn the fourth point, the response must address the interpretation of the selected work as a whole.*
1	**C** Demonstrate sophistication of thought and/or develop a complex literary argument. *This point is based on the argument as a whole, not a single phrase or reference.*

Relevant Skills for Literary Argument Long Essay:

>> General Advice, **see Chapter 4**
>> Long Essay Approaches, **see Chapter 6**
>> Adding Outside Content, **see Chapter 10**
>> Argumentative Essays, **see Chapter 13**

Sample Essay

The prompt for this essay asked students to choose a character from a novel or play who has a significant response to justice or injustice, explain the significance of the search for justice within that work, and analyze the character's search for justice and to what extent it was successful.

In his landmark novel Les Misérables, Victor Hugo casts a critical eye on the social structures and institutions of 19th-century France. His work raises questions about the true nature of justice in a world in which entire classes of citizens are failed by society. While many of the characters seek their vision of a just world, perhaps no character is more deeply affected by the question of justice versus injustice more than the police inspector Javert. Driven in part by his undying devotion to the criminal justice system that Hugo sets out to criticize and in part by a sense of shame in his own family background, Javert is initially unyielding and views morality in black-and-white terms, never considering that his assumptions about good and evil are mistaken. Through his interactions with Jean Valjean, he witnesses mercy and comes to realize that criminal is not the same as evil. His belief in the absolute authority of the law shaken, he is unable to reconcile this new understanding with his rigid principles and ultimately takes his own life.

Throughout much of the novel, Javert's view of justice is simple: justice is dictated by the law, and the law is infallible. While respect for authority and hatred for rebellion are not inherently destructive characteristics, Javert's adoption of both is so extreme that Hugo describes it as "almost evil." He is not a true villain, as his inflexibility and doggedness are well-intentioned, if misguided. His calling to uphold the law is in large part a reaction to his own circumstances: he was born in a prison to a vagabond fortune teller. Javert recognizes deep down that, in this sense, he is no different from the convicts that he guards and is deeply ashamed of this. Based on his family history, he believes that impoverished people are destined to become criminals in order to meet their basic needs, despite the fact that he himself was able to rise above his background. Rather than feeling empathy, he looks down on such people. Javert relishes his position as an officer of the law, considering his duties the ultimate expression of justice and light vanquishing evil.

A — Clearly states the thesis in the intro

Previews what will be discussed in body paragraphs

C — Shows complexity of thought by demonstrating how Javert can be an antagonist without being a villain

Complex (but not convoluted) sentence structure highlights writing skills

Effective use of vocabulary words to show sophistication

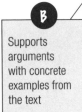

Supports arguments with concrete examples from the text

Includes analysis in the paragraph, not just plot summary

C

More complexity that ties back to previous points

Javert's **lavish fanaticism** for the law prevents him from seeing what the reader is able to see all along through the character of Jean Valjean: that legality does not equal morality, and that goodness can exist within a criminal. To him, it does not matter that Valjean stole a loaf of bread only to feed his starving family—Valjean is a thief and always will be. Furthermore, a person who breaks the law is evil. The intention in doing so is irrelevant, as is any journey to redemption that one might embark on. In Javert's eyes, there is no redemption. His unbending ideals compel him to mete out "justice" in a manner that can verge on cruelty, such as his arrest of the prostitute Fantine. She is obviously in dire circumstances, frantic to get money for her daughter and begging for his mercy. Despite her pleas and protestations that she is a good woman who has fallen on desperate times, Javert is unmoved and orders her to six months in prison. He has seen her commit a crime, however minor, and criminals do not deserve mercy.

Nine years later in Paris, two acts of mercy trigger Javert's reckoning with the concept of justice: the first Valjean's and the second his own. In the June Rebellion of 1832, both men find themselves in the midst of the battle. Javert is taken prisoner after attempting to infiltrate a group of student revolutionaries as a police spy. Valjean, meanwhile, has joined the rebellion in hopes of finding his adopted daughter's suitor, Marius, and has fought valiantly to defend the students' barricade. As a reward, he requests to execute the spy. He leads Javert away and, rather than shooting him, sets him free. In addition, he gives Javert his address to find and arrest him should they both survive the battle. Javert is aghast and confused at the fact that the criminal he has hunted for the better part of twenty years, an "evil" man by his understanding of morality, would show him mercy rather than seize the opportunity to finally be free of him. While it does not deter him from his mission of "justice," this encounter is the first time that Javert perceives a disconnect between moral goodness and the law. He feels a tinge of respect for Valjean. After the insurrection is put down and most of the rebels killed, Valjean rescues the gravely wounded Marius and carries him home through the sewers of Paris. He emerges from the sewers to find Javert waiting to arrest him. Valjean begs him to allow him to return the dying Marius to his grandfather. Javert relents and escorts them to Marius's home and then fulfills Valjean's request to see his daughter one last time. This moment of compassion proves Javert's undoing. Not only has a criminal shown him mercy, but he has shown mercy in return. He has seen such goodness from Valjean that turning him in would be wrong, but letting him go defies Javert's devotion to the law above all else. For the first time, he cannot act both lawfully and morally. "The law" is not "justice." His sense of morality shattered, Javert decides his only option is to remove himself from the situation. His final act is also one of compassion: he writes a letter to his superiors addressing deficiencies in the prison system before plunging into the Seine.

Javert is ultimately destroyed by his own act of mercy. After living his entire life by a black-and-white sense of justice driven by his own background and immovable sense of duty, he cannot accept shades of grey. Through his encounters with Valjean over the course of twenty years that culminate in their confrontation at the barricades, Javert is forced to see that his understanding of the law as beyond reproach is wrong. Goodness, mercy, and love may live outside its bounds. As a character with a rigid sense of morality, Javert is unable to bend to this realization, and so ultimately he breaks.

Recaps the argument in the conclusion

AP FRENCH/GERMAN/ITALIAN/SPANISH LANGUAGE AND CULTURE

Question 1: Email Reply

Suggested Time: 15 minutes (out of 70 minutes total)

Scoring Range: Scored holistically from 0–5 points

Description: You will be asked to read and answer an email message.

RUBRIC	
Scored based on how well you…	• Address all aspects of the prompt and respond to all questions in the original email with detail • Communicate in a clear and understandable manner • Use correct grammar, appropriate vocabulary, and formal register
Description of an essay scoring 4:	These essays maintain the exchange with a response that is generally appropriate within the context of the task. They provide most required information (responses to questions, request for details) with some elaboration. They are fully understandable, with some errors that do not impede comprehensibility. They use varied and generally appropriate vocabulary and idiomatic language. They display general control of grammar, syntax, and usage and generally consistent use of register appropriate for the situation, except for occasional shifts; basic control of cultural conventions appropriate for formal correspondence (e.g., greeting, closing). They include simple, compound, and a few complex sentences.

To earn a 5, add more detail and use more sophisticated vocabulary and grammatical structures.

Relevant Skills for Email Reply:

>> General Advice, **see Chapter 4**
>> Foreign Language Essays, **see Chapter 15**
>> Email Reply Writing, **see Chapter 16**

Sample Essay: See the chapter on Email Reply Writing for specific advice and examples.

Question 2: Argumentative Essay

Suggested Time: 55 minutes (including a 15-minute reading period, out of 70 minutes total)

Scoring Range: Scored holistically from 0–5 points

Description: You will be asked to write an argumentative essay based on 3 sources, including an article; a table, graph, chart, or infographic; and a related audio source (played twice), that present different viewpoints on a topic. You will have access to the print sources and any notes you take on the audio during the entire 40-minute writing period.

RUBRIC		
Scored based on how well you...	**A** Clearly present and defend a position on the topic	
	B Integrate viewpoints from all three sources to support your argument	
	C Organize your essay into clear paragraphs	
	D Use correct grammar and vocabulary	
Description of an essay scoring 4:	These essays include a generally effective treatment of the topic within the context of the task. They demonstrate comprehension of the sources' viewpoints and may include a few inaccuracies. They summarize, with limited integration, content from all three sources in support of an argument and present and defend the student's own viewpoint on the topic with clarity. They develop a persuasive argument with coherence. They are organized with some effective use of transitional elements or cohesive devices and are fully understandable, with some errors that do not impede comprehensibility. They use varied and generally appropriate vocabulary and idiomatic language and have general control of grammar, syntax, and usage. They develop mostly paragraph-length discourse with simple, compound, and a few complex sentences.	

To earn a 5, add more detail, show greater comprehension of the sources, and use more sophisticated vocabulary and grammatical structures.

Relevant Skills for Argumentative Essay:

>> General Advice, **see Chapter 4**
>> Long Essay Approaches, **see Chapter 6**
>> Analyzing Textual Content, **see Chapter 7**
>> Analyzing Quantitative and Graphical Content, **see Chapter 8**
>> Synthesis, **see Chapter 12**
>> Argumentative Essays, **see Chapter 13**
>> Foreign Language Essays, **see Chapter 15**

Sample Essay

Note that this essay is in English as an example of what to do in any of the four languages that use this type of essay. You will write this essay in the language of your test, and the source materials will be in that language.

The prompt for this essay asked whether companies should allow employees to work from home and provided three sources: an article with some facts about working from home, a graph showing perceived pros and cons, and an audio recording about the advantages of remote work.

A

Clearly states a point of view

In general, it's beneficial for a company to permit its employees to work from home. Although there are difficulties (which we've seen in detail during the recent pandemic), the advantages outweigh the disadvantages when it comes to office jobs. For those professions that require hands-on work, such as factories and construction, employees must be kept on site; but with office work there's an increase in productivity, a decrease in expenses, and the opportunity to employ those most qualified without worrying about location, which together give a great competitive advantage to companies ready to adapt to modern times.

Acknowledges an opposing point of view

In the first place, the opportunity to employ those individuals who are most qualified, independent of where they are located, is a big advantage for any business, and an advantage for many employees as well! Though it's true that "There's something magic about sharing lunches… [and] about pitching ideas," as Patrick Pichette says in Source 1, the benefit of having the best person for the job shouldn't be ignored. In the survey referenced in Source 2, this idea is presented as the third most important advantage of working from home. Employees can benefit from social interaction with their coworkers during meetings and other occasions, but their work will be the best if they are the best candidates.

D

Correct use of idiomatic expressions

C

Transitions help guide the flow of ideas, and paragraphs are focused

Similarly, working from home can diminish expenses of various kinds: those of the company, for the maintenance of sites and equipment for employees; those of the personnel, in transportation and food; and, of course, the cost to the environment in vehicle emissions. In the survey referenced in Source 2, "cost savings" ranks as the second most important advantage of working from home. There are public health benefits as well: we can see in 2021 how many companies have protected the health of their employees through the pandemic using only this measure. This can save individuals on their health costs and save businesses on health insurance.

Draws a connection to the real world, which shows comprehension of the issue

Finally, it's important to overcome the impression mentioned by Jennifer Glass in Source 1 "that those who one can see close by are the most productive workers" with the truth that there is an increase in productivity with working from home. In Source 2 an "improvement in productivity" is referenced as the most important advantage of working from home. There are various causes: the time savings that Nuria Amat mentions in Source 3; the reduction in stress that comes with being at home where everything is optimized to one's comfort; the reduction of stress that comes from not having to be in traffic jams every day and having more time for activities such as meditation, exercise (like Nuria Amat), or family activities; the absence of the distractions that abound in a busy workplace. Perhaps reducing the number of meetings to only the essential ones also bolsters this effect.

B

Includes all three sources

Demonstrates understanding of the source material

For all these reasons, I believe that modern companies should consider permitting their employees to telecommute. We live in a new age of technology, and as Margaret Ryan mentions in Source 1, "it's all there, ready and accessible to free us from traveling to work on a daily basis." Since it has so many advantages, why not?

AP JAPANESE LANGUAGE AND CULTURE

Compare-and-Contrast Article

Suggested Time: 20 minutes

Scoring Range: Scored holistically from 0–6 points

Description: You will be asked to write a compare-and-contrast article of 300–400 characters or longer on two related topics or two opposing sides of a single topic.

RUBRIC	
Scored based on how well you...	Ⓐ Identify 3 aspects of the topic Ⓑ Highlight similarities and differences between the two topics or sides Ⓒ Express your preference for a side and explain your reasoning Ⓓ Use correct and appropriate grammar, register, and vocabulary Ⓔ Have a clear organization with transitions
Description of an essay scoring 4:	These essays address all aspects of the prompt, including expression of preference and reasoning, but may lack detail or elaboration. They are generally organized and coherent; use of transitional elements and cohesive devices may be inconsistent. The strained or unnatural flow of expression does not interfere with comprehensibility. There are errors in orthography and mechanics that do not interfere with readability. They may include several mistakes in the use of kanji according to the AP Japanese kanji list. They may include several lapses in otherwise consistent use of register and style appropriate to situation. They include appropriate but limited vocabulary and idioms and appropriate use of grammatical and syntactic structures, but with several errors in complex structures or limited to simple structures.

To earn a 5 or a 6, add more detail, have fewer errors, and use more sophisticated vocabulary and grammatical structures.

Relevant Skills for Compare-and-Contrast Article:

》 General Advice, **see Chapter 4**
》 Long Essay Approaches, **see Chapter 6**
》 Synthesis, **see Chapter 12**
》 Argumentative Essays, **see Chapter 13**
》 Foreign Language Essays, **see Chapter 15**

Sample Essay

Note that we have written the essay in English to better illustrate the features of this essay to all readers, regardless of their level. When you write this essay, you will type it in Japanese using either the *desu/masu* or *da* (plain) style and with kanji where appropriate.

The prompt for this essay asked whether you prefer individual or group projects. It instructed students to compare the two types and list at least three characteristics of each.

Clearly states the preference and follows with reasons

Uses idioms to demonstrate familiarity with the language

Describes aspects of group projects

Draws a comparison between the two formats

Describes aspects of individual projects

Transitions help guide the reader through the various ideas

Concluding sentence sums up the points made and restates the point of view

Between group projects and individual projects, I prefer individual projects. When I am doing a project by myself, I am able to control all aspects of the project. For instance, I can choose when I want to work on it. With a group project, you have to work around other students' schedules. Furthermore, group projects can be a challenge if one or more teammates doesn't work hard. Students who don't complete their share of the project sometimes force a hard-working student to pick up the slack but still earn a good grade thanks to that student, which isn't fair to those who do work hard. With an individual project, the teacher knows that the work reflects you alone, so each student earns the grade he or she deserves.

Group projects do have some benefits, however. Everyone has strengths and weaknesses, and group projects allow people to focus on their strengths. For instance, a project could be split up such that a person who is excellent at writing completes the written portion, a person who loves researching conducts that portion, and someone who is outgoing presents the project to the class. With a group project, if there is a portion of the assignment that you don't like or aren't good at, you may be able to let someone else do it, and you can work on an area that you enjoy and excel at. In a group project, you can also learn from your classmates. They can provide new ideas and help you to improve in the areas that you struggle with. Plus, it can just be more fun working with others instead of alone. Nevertheless, in my opinion the drawbacks outweigh the benefits, and while I don't mind group projects, I prefer working alone.

AP LATIN

Analytical Essay

 Suggested Time: 45 minutes

 Scoring Range: Scored holistically from 0–5 points

Description: You will be asked to analyze the effects of language usage and stylistic features in either 2 Vergil passages, 2 Caesar passages, or 1 Vergil passage and 1 Caesar passage and to support your argument using relevant evidence from the texts and readings in English.

RUBRIC		
Scored based on how well you...	**A**	Articulate a defensible claim or thesis
	B	Analyze the effects of language use and stylistic features in Latin texts
	C	Support the argument using relevant evidence from Latin texts and readings in English
	D	Use reasoning to draw conclusions and make inferences based on textual features
	E	Use contextual knowledge and references to support the analysis
Description of an essay scoring 4:		These essays answer the prompt, providing main ideas and some supporting details. Although the analysis may not be nuanced, it is based on a sound understanding of the Latin. They provide examples of Latin that are generally accurate, specific, and relevant, properly cited; while not plentiful, the citations are drawn from throughout both passages. They make some inferences and draw some conclusions that accurately reflect the Latin and support the analysis. They may rely only on what is stated, or may make inaccurate inferences. They use some specific contextual references that support the analysis.

To earn a 5, add more examples from both passages, have fewer errors, and use more inferences and draw stronger conclusions to support the analysis.

Relevant Skills for Analytical Essay:

» General Advice, **see Chapter 4**
» Long Essay Approaches, **see Chapter 6**
» Analyzing Textual Content, **see Chapter 7**
» Synthesis, **see Chapter 12**

Sample Essay

The prompt for this essay provided two excerpts from the Aeneid, one in which Aeneas sees Helen and one in which he sees Dido, and asked students to analyze his reactions to both.

Thesis high-lights similarities and differences between the excerpts

Aeneas has vastly different reactions to his encounter with Helen versus Dido. However, despite one being a reaction of anger and the other of love, both encounters serve to show more of Aeneas' character and his values.

Clearly addresses Aeneas' reaction to Helen and links it with the accompanying text

Aeneas' initial reaction to encountering Helen is of pure rage ("Exarsere ignes animo" A Line 1) and described as "fires burning in his soul." He despises Helen for her role in the fall of Troy, his home and that of his people. Instead of recognizing Helen as a queen, he actually questions whether she deserves such a title ("partoque ibit regina tri-umpho" A Line 4). The question being "will she depart as a queen?", in other words—does the woman to blame for the fall of Troy deserve such a title? After all, he questions whether her existence was to only cause Troy to burn ("Troia arserit igni?" A Line 7). Furthermore, Aeneas actually sees Helen as an evil woman ("exstinxisse nefas tamen" A Line 11) describing that killing Helen would be "extinguishing an evil" and an honor to the Trojan deaths. His reaction demonstrates his devo-tion to his homeland and his people. Though he recognizes that there is no honor in killing a woman ("habet haec victoria laudem" A Line 10), he believes that avenging his people will bring him praise ("lauda-bor poenas" A Line 12). Upon encountering Helen, Aeneas' character demonstrates his devotion to country and duty. He would be willing to commit a crime of murder when it came to the woman to blame for the fall of Troy and the death of his people.

Demonstrates understanding of the text by providing context

Demonstrates awareness of both the literal translation and the meaning of the text

Includes additional points to support the argument. This evidence serves to elaborate on the use of the word "regina," also used in passage B.

As part of the analysis, this point serves as the common evidence found in both passages

In contrast, Aeneas shows a different character upon encountering Dido. His initial reaction is both despair and regret. He questions whether it was his fault that she took her life ("funeris heu tibi causa fui?" B Line 3). Accepting of this fault, he seeks to explain to Dido that he did not leave willingly. Instead, his devotion to his home and people was the cause of his departure ("invitus, regina, tuo de litore cessi" B Line 5). He also demonstrates his devotion to Dido herself by calling her queen and swearing upon the stars ("Per sidera iuro" B Line 3) that he "left her shores unwillingly." Again, he demonstrates his devotion to his people by obeying the commands of the gods ("sed me iussa deum" B Line 6). The gods had commanded that he leave her shores to find a new home for people. In this encounter, Aeneas attempts to explain the importance of that duty, which outweighed his devotion to Dido. However, this explanation is not enough for Dido, as she turns away from Aeneas, prompting him to call out for her to stay ("Siste gradum" B Line 10). Aeneas is desperate to spend one last moment with Dido, for such a chance was only allowed by fate ("Extremum fato quod te adloquor hoc est" B Line 11). For Aeneas, this is his final goodbye to Dido, in which he demonstrates his continued love for her while still remaining true to his duty and piety.

Aeneas has two very different views of Helen and Dido, one of hate and the other of love. The passages demonstrate the rage he feels toward Helen for the fall of Troy and the devotion he had toward Dido. Though the feelings expressed in the encounters are different, his piety and devotion to his people remain the same. It is the reason he would seek to avenge his people by killing Helen and the reason he had to unwillingly leave Dido.

Uses the Latin evidence to continue the point of common ground between the two passages—the devotion Aeneas has to his people

Refers back to the previous usage of "regina" in terms of Helen and demonstrates the difference in meaning when used in the context with Dido

Continuation of the thesis statement, providing an analysis of Aeneas' devotion

A concluding statement that references the differences and similarities between the texts

AP SPANISH LITERATURE AND CULTURE

Questions 1–2: Short Essays

Suggested Time: 15 minutes each (out of 100 minutes total)

Scoring Range: 0–3 points in Content (answering the question correctly) and 0–3 points in Language (Spanish fluency), for each short essay

Description:

❑ One Text Explanation will ask you to read an excerpt from a text on the required reading list, identify the author and period of the text, and explain the development of a given theme found within the excerpt in relation to the whole work from which the excerpt is taken.

❑ One Text and Art Comparison will ask you to read an excerpt from a text on the required reading list and study an image of a work of art (e.g., a painting, photograph, sculpture, or drawing) related by theme to the text. You will be asked to compare how a particular theme is represented in both the text and the image, and then to connect that theme to the genre, period, or movement of the text.

RUBRIC
How to Earn Points
The prompt will provide 3 tasks for each short-answer question. You'll earn a point for each task that is completed correctly.

Relevant Skills for Short Essays:

> » General Advice, **see Chapter 4**
> » Short Answer Approaches, **see Chapter 5**
> » Analyzing Textual Content, **see Chapter 7**
> » Analyzing Quantitative and Graphical Content, **see Chapter 8**
> » Foreign Language Essays, **see Chapter 15**

Question 3: Analysis of a Single Text

Suggested Time: 35 minutes (out of 100 minutes total)

Scoring Range: Scored holistically from 0–5 points in each of two areas, Content and Language Usage

Description: You will be asked to read an excerpt from a text on the required reading list and then analyze how the text represents the characteristics of a particular genre as well as a particular historical, cultural, or social context.

RUBRIC		
	Content	**Language Usage**
Scored based on how well you...	**A** Analyze how characteristics of the text represent the specified subgenre **B** Analyze how cultural products, practices, or perspectives found in the text reflect the given cultural context **C** Discuss a variety of rhetorical, stylistic, or structural features in the text **D** Include a thesis statement and have a logical structure **E** Use specific examples from the text to support the analysis	• Use varied and appropriate vocabulary • Present main ideas, supporting ideas, and nuances • Use correct and effective grammatical and sentence structures; use transitions to guide understanding • Follow Spanish writing conventions correctly

RUBRIC		
	Content	**Language Usage**
Description of an essay scoring 4:	These essays describe characteristics of the text that represent the specified technique and cultural products, practices, or perspectives of the given cultural context found in the text. They describe some rhetorical, stylistic, or structural features in the text. They include a statement of purpose, evidence of organization (a stated topic, an introduction, a conclusion), and a logical progression of ideas. They elaborate on main points and support observations with examples; however, the examples may not always be clear and relevant. They contain some errors of interpretation, but errors do not detract from the overall quality of the essay.	The vocabulary is appropriate to the text(s) being discussed and presents main ideas and some supporting details. The control of grammatical and syntactic structures is good; occasional errors in the use of verb tenses and moods do not detract from understanding; word order and formation are mostly accurate. Writing conventions (e.g., spelling, accent marks, punctuation, paragraphing) are generally accurate; occasional errors do not detract from understanding. Paragraphing shows grouping and progression of ideas.
To earn a 5, use stronger analysis, include better textual examples, add nuance to your analysis, and write in a way that has fewer errors and is more sophisticated.		

Relevant Skills for Analysis of a Single Text:

» General Advice, **see Chapter 4**

» Long Essay Approaches, **see Chapter 6**

» Rhetorical Analysis, **see Chapter 11**

» Foreign Language Essays, **see Chapter 15**

Sample Essay

The prompt for this essay provided an excerpt from Conde Lucanor and asked students to explain how it fits in its subgenre of* el exemplo didáctico medieval *and its cultural context.

En <u>Libro del Conde Lucanor</u>, Don Juan Manuel nos da una obra representante de las características de la literatura española medieval y el contexto sociocultural de la España del siglo XIV. Es una obra didáctica y moralizante, y también muestra ritmos y estructuras que reflejan raíces en la tradición oral que caracterizaba esa época en que pocos pudieran leer. El cuento "De lo que aconteció a un mozo que casó con una mujer muy fuerte y muy brava" específicamente usa hipérbole para comunicar una moraleja que tiene mucho que ver con el machismo y las relaciones de poder entre hombre y mujer.

B

Puts the work into a broader context

D

Clearly introduces the subject of the paragraph

El propósito del cuento es transmitir la moraleja, que se resume al fin como "Si al comienzo no muestras quién eres nunca podrás después, cuando quisieres." En contexto de la historia del cuento, significa que el hombre debe dominar su esposa del comienzo de su relación, para mantenerla suficientemente obediente y dócil. Como todos los cuentos en ese parte del libro, este empieza con el Conde Lucanor, quien solicita consejo de su consejero Patronio. Patronio da su ayuda tras un cuento (dentro del cuento), y así desarolla la moraleja. La forma del cuento refleja las características de la literatura española medieval: usa hipérbole (el mozo amenaza su esposa diciendo que va a matar a todos que no hagan lo que manda), humor (los acciones dramáticos del esposo) y la estructura de un cuento dentro de un cuento para cautivar al lector y comunicar el mensaje. Estas formas provienen de la tradición oral y reflejan la idea del cuento como instrumento para enseñar.

C

Points out specific rhetorical devices and explains how they are used

A

Relates the text to the specified subgenre

Además de las características didácticas y moralizantes, el cuento también revela el contexto sociocultural en que fue escrito, sobre todo de la construcción del genero y las relaciones interpersonales. Patronio recomienda al Conde, tras su cuento, que su pariente no debe casarse con la mujer violenta sino que puede controlarla. Los roles de género que presenta son más o menos "un hombre debe mandar en su casa" y "la mujer debe ser obediente y dócil." Las personajes del cuento aceptan como necesario el uso de violencia y manipulación para conseguir la sumisión de la mujer. Adicionalmente, el cuento nos imparta información sobre la diversidad cultural de España en el siglo XIV, en particular las diferencias entre los españoles y los árabes que dominaban parte de la territoria de España durante esa época. Como el escritor nos dice específicamente que este mancebo es de ascendencia moro, es posible que la violencia cómica con que se comporta sirve como estereotipo racial que indica como los españoles consideraron a los árabes, y que

Uses transitions to aid in the flow of ideas

E

Provides and explains specific details of the text

el conclusión—que el pariente no debe casarse con la mujer si no va a actuar como el mancebo—insinua que solo un árabe actuaría con tanta violencia, mientras un español haría mejor en conseguir una esposa más dócil.

En conclusión, en <u>Conde Lucanor, Exemplo XXXV</u> ("De lo que aconteció a un mozo que casó con una mujer muy fuerte y muy brava"), don Juan Manuel usa las características del exemplo didáctico medieval para transmitir la moraleja que un esposa debe dominar a su esposa. También muestra el contexto sociocultural de la España del siglo XIV—los roles de genero prescritos y la actitud de los españoles hacia los árabes con quienes vivían lado a lado.

Uses idioms to demonstrate fluency

Question 4: Text Comparison

Suggested Time: 35 minutes (out of 100 minutes total)

Scoring Range: Scored holistically from 0–5 points in each of two areas, Content and Language Usage

Description: You will be asked to read 2 excerpts related by theme—one from a text on the required list, the other from a text not on the list—and analyze the effect of literary devices that the authors use in the texts to develop a particular theme that is provided in the prompt.

RUBRIC		
	Content	**Language Usage**
Scored based on how well you...	**A** Analyze literary devices in both texts **B** Analyze the development of a theme in both texts **C** Include a thesis statement and have a clear structure and progression of ideas **D** Support analysis with specific textual examples	• Use varied and appropriate vocabulary • Present main ideas, supporting ideas, and nuances • Use correct and effective grammatical and sentence structures, use transitions to guide understanding • Follow Spanish writing conventions correctly
Description of an essay scoring 4:	These essays discuss rhetorical, stylistic, or structural features in both texts in relation to the development of the theme. They explain and compare the presence of the theme in the texts. They include an explicit statement of purpose (thesis), a coherent structure, and a logical progression of ideas. They support their analysis with appropriate textual examples.	The vocabulary is appropriate to the text(s) being discussed and presents main ideas and some supporting details. The control of grammatical and syntactic structures is good; occasional errors in the use of verb tenses and moods do not detract from understanding; word order and formation are mostly accurate. Writing conventions (e.g., spelling, accent marks, punctuation, paragraphing) are generally accurate; occasional errors do not detract from understanding; paragraphing shows grouping and progression of ideas.

To earn a 5, use stronger analysis, include better textual examples, add nuance to your analysis, and write in a way that has fewer errors and is more sophisticated.

Relevant Skills for Text Comparison:

» General Advice, **see Chapter 4**
» Long Essay Approaches, **see Chapter 6**
» Rhetorical Analysis, **see Chapter 11**
» Synthesis, **see Chapter 12**
» Foreign Language Essays, **see Chapter 15**

Sample Essay

The prompt for this essay provided two poems and asked students to analyze the rhetorical devices that the poems use to develop the theme of patriarchy.

Tanto el poema "A Julia de Burgos" por Julia de Burgos como "Tú me quieres blanca" por Alfonsina Storni utilizan los recursos literarios para desarollar el tema del sistema patriarcal. En ambos poemas las escritoras representan contrastes entre lo que hay en la alma de una mujer y lo que ha impuesto el mundo social y el sistema patriarcal. En esta manera, señalan como es ese sistema y lo contrasten de la imagen de una mujer libre de sus limitaciones.

En "A Julia de Burgos" la poeta usa el desdoblamiento para hacer el contraste: hay dos Julias de Burgos y la "yo" del poema representa la mujer verdadera, libre, mientras la "tú" representa la imagen social de la mujer, delimitada por las expectativas de la sociedad. La imagen social tiene que ser falsa, hipócrita, y pintada; también tiene que ser sumisa, no manda a si misma sino que está dirigida por fuerzas externas como el marido, los padres y muchas cosas más. Burgos usa yuxtaposición repetida (Tú... yo no; Tú... yo no) y enumeración para indicar las diferencias entre la persona internal sin restricciones y la imagen que es "muñeca de mentira social." En esta manera el lector gane un idea del sistema patriarcal definido por limitaciones.

C
Begins with a thesis statement that establishes the points that will be discussed

D
References and explains specific aspects of the text

A

States and explains specific rhetorical strategies used in the text

B

Compares the two literary sources

"Tú me quieres blanca", en vez de contraste dos versiones de la misma persona, hace contraste entre la voz del poema y el "tú" que tiene tantas expectativas. El "tú" en este poema es sin duda masculino, y el poema incluye censura por lo que él puede hacer mientras la mujer tiene que cumplir una norma de pureza inalcanzable. Storni usa metafora para compararse a si misma (la voz) con elementos de la naturaleza para dar las impresiones de pureza; entonces usa más metaforas para mandar purificarse al "tú" que tiene tantas demandas. El sistema patriarcal, en este caso, va definido por expectativas: "Tú me quieres nívea, tú me quieres blanca, tú me quieres alba." La repetición refuerza la imagen y da la impresión de agotarle a uno. No hay escapa.

"A Julia de Burgos" y "Tú me quieres blanca" llaman la atención al impacto que el sistema patriarcal tiene en una mujer y los dos utilizan los recursos literarios para dar una impresión concreta de ese impacto en su vida interna. Las dos poetas Burgos y Storni ilustran una imagen en que la mujer libre se irrita bajo las expectativas y restricciones del sistema patriarcal.

Concluding thought makes the essay sound complete

Chapter 3

Admissions Exams

ACT

Argumentative Essay

Time Limit: 40 minutes

Scoring Range: Two graders each provide a score from 1–6 in four different categories. The average scores for each grader are added together to yield an overall score from 2–12.

Description: You will be asked to read a prompt and write an essay in which you develop your own perspective on an issue based on three provided perspectives and any viewpoints of your own.

RUBRIC			
	Ideas and Analysis	**Development and Support**	**Organization**	**Language Use and Conventions**

| Scored based on how well you... | **A** Understand the issue given, the purpose for writing, and the audience   **B** Generate relevant ideas | **C** Explain and explore your ideas   **D** Discuss implications   **E** Illustrate through examples | **F** Organize the essay in a way that clearly shows the relationship between ideas   **G** Guide the reader through the discussion | **H** Use correct grammar, syntax, word usage, and mechanics   **I** Have an appropriate style and tone for the audience |

Two graders will each score your essay holistically on each of the following areas, based on your essay as a whole.

Relevant Skills for Argumentative Essay:

>> General Advice, **see Chapter 4**
>> Long Essay Approaches, **see Chapter 6**
>> Adding Outside Content, **see Chapter 10**
>> Synthesis, **see Chapter 12**
>> Argumentative Essays, **see Chapter 13**

Sample Essay

The prompt for this essay asked about the implications of adults enjoying things that used to be only for children. Perspective 1 says that understanding "kid stuff" helps adults understand children, Perspective 2 argues that adults should be mature role models instead, and Perspective 3 contends that adults harm kids by invading their spaces.

While the name "children's entertainment" implies that the entertainment should only be enjoyed by children, that assumption is incorrect. Entertainment that is created for adult audiences uses the same types of media that children's entertainment uses, like animation and video games. Shows and movies that are created for children can also explore ideas and stories that are of interest to adults. In addition, adults may like to engage with media that reminds them of their own childhoods. The classification of a large group of media (animated shows, video games, and collectibles) as children's entertainment ignores the variety of audiences for that media as well as the numerous reasons adults may engage with it.

A

Provides context to show that the author understands the issue

Many kinds of media that are used for children's entertainment can be used for adult audiences. Animated TV shows and films, along with video games, are not only created for children. Shows ranging from South Park to The Midnight Gospel use animation to entertain and discuss themes and ideas relevant to adults. Many video games are rated mature and are not suitable for children to play. Categorizing any animated show or video game as entertainment for children ignores the variety of content and audiences that those shows and games may have. Although shows and games may look similar to children's entertainment, it does not mean that those shows and games are childish.

E

Illustrates the argument using examples from real life

B/D

Concedes one point but refutes another, which demonstrates complexity

F

Each body paragraph is focused around one clear point

H/I

Incorporates precise word usage and uses a formal, academic tone

Incorporates Perspective 1

Incorporates Perspective 3

Additionally, entertainment that is created for children can be enjoyable for both kids and adults. Much of children's media today is much more complex than the cartoons of decades ago. One of the most popular cartoons of the twenty-first century is Avatar: The Last Airbender. That show does depict some classic tropes of children's shows, like silly adventures and fun animals. It also explores issues like war, imperialism, redemption, and justice. Shows like Avatar appeal to both children and adults, complicating the idea that children's shows are just for kids. Children's entertainment can be immature or ridiculous, but that is reductive, and implying that people who enjoy children's shows are immature or poor role models does not take into consideration the content of children's shows. In fact, many children's shows are designed with a family audience in mind, as parents and guardians are likely to watch shows and movies with their children. Having a show or movie people of all ages can enjoy allows families to spend time together, even if the adults and children are enjoying it for different reasons.

Furthermore, generalizing adults as immature or childish for enjoying children's entertainment misses one of the biggest reasons adults may engage with "childish" things: nostalgia. Many adults who buy collectibles or read comics are connecting with the things that they enjoyed as children. Two of the biggest franchises in entertainment, Disney and Marvel, have been around for decades, long enough for the children who first enjoyed those things to become adults. Although there is concern that adults will take over children's cultural space, there are few reasons for adults to engage with entertainment that is designed exclusively for children. Educational programs and shows geared to young children, like Sesame Street or Paw Patrol, are less appealing to adults. Instead, adults are drawn to what they liked as children.

Children's entertainment is a vast and complex category. Simply looking at the type of media is not enough to decide if something is for children or adults, as shown by the large number of animated shows exclusively for adults. Entertainment that is designed for children can also be enjoyed by adults, whether it is because the adults are spending time with their children or they're reminded of their own childhoods. Children's entertainment is not only for children.

Good use of transition to guide the reader through the author's points

Incorporates Perspective 2

Includes counter-examples to strengthen the argument and show multiple implications

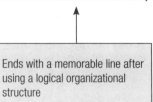

Ends with a memorable line after using a logical organizational structure

ISEE

Personal Essay

Time Limit: 30 minutes

Scoring Range: Unscored; essay will be sent to the school(s) you apply to

Description: You will be asked to write an essay in response to a simple, general prompt, which will ask something about your life, personality, or values.

Rubric: This essay is unscored, so there is no specific rubric. However, while every school may be looking for slightly different attributes in students who apply, we can provide some suggestions to make your essay show off the best parts of you for any school that you apply to. In your essay, you should try to show that you are:

RUBRIC	
Personal Attributes	**Writing Skills**
• Interested in learning • Motivated and have a positive attitude • Intelligent, not childish or silly • Thoughtful, kind, self-reflective, and likeable	• Well-versed in English vocabulary, grammar, punctuation, and mechanics • Able to organize an essay into multiple, focused paragraphs • Able to explain your thinking

Relevant Skills for Personal Essay:

» General Advice, **see Chapter 4**
» Long Essay Approaches, **see Chapter 6**
» Adding Outside Content, **see Chapter 10**
» Personal Essays, **see Chapter 14**

Sample Essay

The prompt for this essay asked the student to describe a favorite teacher and what the student admires about the teacher.

My favorite teacher is Mrs. Gage. She was my teacher in 6th grade, and even though that was two years ago, I still have good memories of being in her class. Mrs. Gage was always patient and kind with everyone in the class.

Shows interest in learning

One of the things that I really liked about Mrs. Gage was that she would let me read at my desk when I finished assignments early. I read so many books that year! We had vocabulary quizzes in class every week, and I usually finished mine pretty quickly, so I'm glad that I was allowed to read after I checked over my work. Sometimes one of the words from the quiz would even show up in the book that I was reading, which made me extra thankful that Mrs. Gage had assigned that word.

Demonstrates enthusiasm

Shows likeability

I also enjoyed having Mrs. Gage as my teacher because she's led a very exciting life. She has an excellent singing voice and once performed in a musical on Broadway. She also used to live in Paris and would talk about her adventures finding bakeries with fabulous croissants and strolling through all of the wonderful museums there. She knows how to speak French really well, which inspired me to learn that language so that I will be able to communicate with people when I visit France. I just started learning French this year, and sometimes when I stop by her classroom at my old elementary school on my walk home from my current school, she'll help me practice by having a conversation in French with me.

Shows relationship-building

Conclusion sums up the main focus of the essay

I am so lucky to have had Mrs. Gage as my teacher because I have learned so much from her, and she has encouraged me to read more and to study new things. I hope that my younger sister has her as a teacher next year!

Shows positivity

SSAT

Personal Essay Topic

Time Limit: 25 minutes

Scoring Range: Unscored; essay will be sent to the school(s) you apply to

Description: You will be given a choice between the personal essay topic and the general essay topic. The personal topic will provide a brief prompt asking you a question related to yourself and your values.

RUBRIC
How to Earn Points
See the rubric information for the ISEE essay.

Relevant Skills for Personal Essay Topic:
» General Advice, **see Chapter 4**
» Long Essay Approaches, **see Chapter 6**
» Adding Outside Content, **see Chapter 10**
» Personal Essays, **see Chapter 14**

Sample Essay

The prompt for this essay asked where you would go if you could travel anywhere in the world for a week.

If I could choose anywhere in the world to go for one week, I would go to France. There are so many things to do and see in France, and a trip there would give me the opportunity to practice speaking French.

Thoughtful and academically oriented

I would start my trip in Paris, where I would visit the Louvre Museum and the Eiffel Tower. At the Louvre, I would like to see the Mona Lisa, though my friend who visited last year said that the room it's in gets really crowded. Hopefully I'll be able to get close enough to admire the masterpiece. Even if I don't, there is lots of other amazing art there to see. I'd also like to challenge myself to climb up the stairs in the Eiffel tower. It might be faster to take the elevator, but I think I'll want to be able to stop and admire the views of the city on my way up.

Optimistic outlook

Willingness to take on challenges

In addition to spending time in Paris, I would like to see Monet's gardens in Giverny. My mom took me to the Monet exhibit that came to the art museum near my house a few months ago, and Monet's paintings were some of the most beautiful paintings I've ever seen. I would very much like to see the inspiration for Monet's work. Maybe I can even try my hand at painting.

Topic sentences make the focus of each paragraph clear

Thoughtful and likeable

To top off the trip, I'd have to make sure I had some delicious French food. I'd definitely want to have croissants for breakfast and crepes with chocolate and banana for afternoon snacks. If I'm feeling adventurous, I might even try escargot! It would be a wonderful trip, but I think I'd need to go back some day to see more. I bet I could spend a week in the Louvre alone.

Open to new things

General Essay Topic

Time Limit: 25 minutes

Scoring Range: Unscored; essay will be sent to the school(s) you apply to

Description: You will be given a choice between the personal essay topic and the general essay topic. The general topic will ask for your opinion on an issue that any student could respond to.

RUBRIC
How to Earn Points
See the rubric information for the ISEE essay.

Relevant Skills for General Essay Topic:

>> General Advice, **see Chapter 4**
>> Long Essay Approaches, **see Chapter 6**
>> Adding Outside Content, **see Chapter 10**

Sample Essay

The prompt for this essay asked about the characteristics of a good teacher.

A good teacher is someone who knows how to explain things, knows how to listen, and knows how to make learning fun. Knowing how to explain things is important because not everybody learns the same way, and sometimes it's not enough for a teacher to just tell you that something is true. It's also important for teachers to listen to what students are saying so that the teachers know when we don't understand. Finally, it is much easier to stay motivated when learning difficult material when there is fun involved.

Shows thought-fulness and perspective

One example that comes to mind is my math teacher, Ms. Fort. When she was teaching my class about exponent rules, she explained them in several different ways, and even gave us a memory trick, MADSPM, to help us remember. Now every time I think of exponents, I think of the silly way she talked about MADSPM, and I remember the rules!

Good organization

Interest in learning

Another example is my history teacher, Mr. Richey. Not only does he tell lots of stories, which makes historical events come alive, but he also encourages us to ask lots of questions. He makes us feel like he is interested in what students have to say by involving us in discussion. This year we're learning U.S. History, and he and some of the other 8th grade teachers organized a trip for us to Washington, D.C. next month so that we can actually see what Congress and the Senate are like first-hand. I am really looking forward to the trip. By making sure we learn things through experience and not just out of a book, he makes learning fun.

Good organization

Interest in learning

I have been fortunate to learn from many good teachers, and I hope that if I become a teacher someday, I will be a good teacher with all three of these characteristics.

Conclusion sums up the point of the essay

TOEFL

Integrated Writing Task

Time Limit: 20 minutes

Scoring Range: Scored holistically from 0–5

Description: You will be asked to read a short passage and listen to a short lecture, then write in response to what you read and listened to.

RUBRIC
How to Earn Points
You'll be scored on how well you summarize the important points from both the passage and the lecture as well as on the correctness of your English language writing.

Relevant Skills for Integrated Writing Task:

>> General Advice, **see Chapter 4**
>> Long Essay Approaches, **see Chapter 6**
>> Analyzing Textual Content, **see Chapter 7**
>> Synthesis, **see Chapter 12**
>> Foreign Language Essays, **see Chapter 15**

Independent Writing Task

Time Limit: 30 minutes

Scoring Range: Scored holistically from 0–5

Description: You will be asked to write an essay based on personal experience or opinion in response to a writing topic.

RUBRIC	
Scored based on how well you...	**A** Address the topic and task **B** Organize your essay and explain your points **C** Demonstrate coherence and follow a clear progression **D** Demonstrate English fluency through the use of vocabulary, idioms, and a variety of sentence structures
Description of an essay scoring 4:	These essays address the topic and task well, though some points may not be fully elaborated; are generally well organized and well developed, using appropriate and sufficient explanations, exemplifications and/or details; and display unity, progression and coherence, though they may contain occasional redundancy, digression, or unclear connections. They display facility in the use of language, demonstrating syntactic variety and range of vocabulary, though they will probably have occasional noticeable minor errors in structure, word form, or use of idiomatic language that do not interfere with meaning.

To earn a 5, add more details and explanations, stay on topic, reduce errors, and use more sophisticated vocabulary and sentence structures.

Relevant Skills for Independent Writing Task:

>> General Advice, **see Chapter 4**
>> Long Essay Approaches, **see Chapter 6**
>> Adding Outside Content, **see Chapter 10**
>> Argumentative Essays, **see Chapter 13**
>> Foreign Language Essays, **see Chapter 15**

Sample Essay

The prompt for this essay asked about the best way to quickly get to know a new city as a visitor.

A — Clear response to the question

B — Body paragraph has a clear focus and includes a specific example

C — Transition helps with the flow of ideas, and topic sentences are used to set up the point of each paragraph

D — Idioms demonstrate facility with English

Introduces the reasoning that will be used

I believe that the best way to get to know a city that I am visiting for the first time is to take a food tour. Food tours are an ideal way to get to know new places in a way that goes beyond the superficial because they give you the opportunity to get to know areas that go beyond the typical tourist locations and experience the types of foods that people in that city eat.

One reason I believe that food tours are the best way to get to know a new city is that the tour will often take you into parts of the city that you might not otherwise know to explore. For example, when I participated in a food tour in Lima, Peru, my tour guide took me to a wonderful outdoor market. The market was bustling with locals and gave me a good feel for what it might be like to live in Lima and do my food shopping there. While the market seemed to be very popular with people who live in Lima, it was far from my hotel and was not mentioned in any of my tourist books. Without the food tour, I would not have known of its existence.

In addition, food tours are an excellent opportunity to try new foods that are enjoyed in that city. When I participated in a food tour in Honolulu, Hawaii, I was able to taste lots of different goods that I'd never been exposed to at home. One particularly unique food was Spam musubi—a snack made with sushi rice, Spam, and soy sauce that is wrapped in nori sheets. It was delicious, and a combination that never would have occurred to me! I also got to try fresh pineapple coated in li hing mui powder, a salty, sweet, and sour combination that was unlike anything I'd tasted before. There were so many delicious foods, and the food tour really expanded my palate.

Food tours are the best way to get to know a new city in a short amount of time because they provide a number of different ways to interact with the city that go beyond merely visiting well-known tourist attractions. Not only do you get to experience parts of the city that are lesser known to tourists and foods that are unique to the city, but you typically get to do it with a local as your guide. People frequently say that the way to a person's heart is through that person's stomach, and I think the same is true when getting to know a new city.

Conclusion recaps the thesis and reasoning

Concluding thought ties the essay together

PART B

SKILL CHAPTERS

Chapter 4

General Advice

Applicable to: All essays

Goals

In this chapter, you will learn how to:

- use prewriting to produce a cohesive essay
- add sophistication to boost your essay score
- fulfill the requirements of a rubric
- plan parts of your essay before test day

SO YOU WANT TO WRITE AN ESSAY...

We'll begin by going over some general strategies for just about any standardized test essay, long or short, that you will write. Remember that these differ from most other essays you'll write primarily in terms of their time limits. You will need to have a good idea of how to write a solid essay, but you'll also need a strategy for how to manage your time so that you aren't hurriedly ending your essay mid-sentence when the timer runs out. As with most things in life, your essay will be most effective if you start with a plan.

THE KEY TO A TOP-SCORING ESSAY: PREWRITING

Throughout your school career, you have likely learned many strategies for planning out your writing, whether you were assigned a paragraph or a long research paper. A couple of examples that may be familiar are idea webs and outlines. With both of these systems, you can begin by deciding on the biggest points you want to make and then jotting down some of the key details that will support your points.

 Regardless of your preferred method, prewriting should be a part of any essay test you take.

Any essay scorer will tell you that it's easy to identify an essay whose writer did not plan beforehand; such essays typically begin making one point and end with an entirely different argument. Or, the grader is left wondering until the conclusion what the author's point is, because the author did not state it clearly until the end. These types of essays are certain to earn a low score, regardless of the test. When you just start writing without a plan in mind, you will find yourself developing your ideas as you write. This can be fine for a journal entry, but for a formal essay, the reader should know right away what your argument is, and you should spend the whole essay clarifying that argument, rather than talking through your ideas, hoping you'll reach some kind of point by the end.

Having a cohesive essay isn't the only reason to prewrite. You'll find the writing process much faster and easier if you have a plan for what you want to say. This will allow you to use your limited time efficiently and help avoid the feeling of being stuck and unsure of what else to write.

HOW TO MANAGE YOUR TIME

Whatever the time limit for your essay, plan to spend some time prewriting. For short-answer questions, this may be as little as 30 seconds that you spend jotting down a quick answer to each question before writing your answer in complete sentences. For essays that have a time limit of 30 minutes or more, plan to spend at least 5 minutes prewriting. Then you'll spend the bulk of the remaining time writing the essay. For long essays, try to save 3–5 minutes at the end to proofread.

Let's start by discussing how to spend your prewriting time for longer essays. When you open your essay prompt, start by reading all parts of the prompt. You may find it helpful to underline parts the question or key aspects of source materials that are included. You may also jot down notes as you read to help you stay focused and begin to gather your thoughts.

Next, start to plan out your essay in your test booklet, scratch paper, or provided planning pages. In the next two chapters on short and long essay approaches, you'll learn some specific structures you may use for your essay. If your essay has multiple paragraphs, as all longer essays will, make a plan for the focus of each paragraph. This way, when you are writing, you will know what to write about in each paragraph, and you'll know when to start and end each paragraph. You may find it helpful to write down some brief notes about what points you want to be sure to make in each paragraph, or you may feel comfortable simply jotting down the topic of the paragraph. Either way, write down your plan! It's also a good idea to write down your thesis statement, which is the overall point of your essay. We'll talk much more about the thesis statement later on, but it's crucial that you know your main argument before writing your essay.

Before you start writing, reread the prompt and check that you have accounted for all aspects of what it is asking you to do. For instance, if the prompt asks you to address certain viewpoints or certain textual materials, make sure that you have included all of them in your outline. Be sure that your thesis statement answers the question that is asked in the prompt.

PREWRITING STEPS

1. ▶ Read and annotate the question and any included documents.

2. ▶ Write down your thesis statement.

3. ▶ Plan out the focus of each paragraph.

4. ▶ Double check that you have addressed all parts of the prompt in your plans.

STRUCTURE, GENERALLY SPEAKING

No matter its length, every essay needs a beginning, middle, and end. If your essay lacks a thoughtful structure, your thoughts may seem to just continue without any sense of ending one point and beginning another, which can be difficult for a reader to follow. As previously mentioned, planning the focus of each paragraph makes it easier to know when to start a new paragraph.

Each body paragraph also needs a beginning, middle, and end. Generally speaking, you want to introduce the example or argument that is the focus of that paragraph, provide lots of details that tie the topic back to your thesis statement, and then conclude the point you are making in the paragraph. A paragraph should never begin in the middle of a point, assuming the reader is familiar with your topic, nor should it end by going off in a different direction that is unrelated to the point in that paragraph.

THE STRUCTURE OF A PARAGRAPH

1. ▶ If it is not the first body paragraph, begin with a transition to move smoothly from the previous topic.

2. ▶ Introduce the focus of the paragraph.

3. ▶ Write details to explain your argument or example and show how it supports your thesis.

4. ▶ Wrap up the point of the paragraph and restate your argument and/or transition into the next paragraph.

CAN YOU TALK GOOD?

Beyond having a logical structure, your essay must also have correct punctuation, grammar, and spelling, as well as an appropriate tone. Regardless of whether your essay is in English or in a foreign language, the grader wants to see that you understand the mechanics of the language, including tense, subject-verb agreement, and proper punctuation and spelling. Of course, these aspects of your writing will be even more important in language-based essays. Refer to the rubric for each essay to see how much mechanics factor into your score; in some cases, this is an explicit component of the scoring.

These writing skills aren't important just when they are part of the rubric, however. The rules exist for a reason. If you do not follow the rules of written English (or whatever language your essay is in), the grader may not understand, or may misunderstand, what you are trying to say. For instance, if you write *The governor's policies* when you really mean *The governors' policies*, you could actually lose points on the content portion of the rubric if you are incorrectly referring to just one governor when you meant to refer to multiple. And if you make enough errors, your essay can be challenging to read and understand, which will harm your score as well.

To prepare for your essay, it may be helpful to turn off auto-correct and spell check on any devices you tend to write on. Even if you are taking a computer-based test (more on that later), you won't have these aids to help you identify and correct mistakes. If you normally rely on them, you'll want to practice finding and correcting errors yourself. If your essay test is on paper, try not to write so quickly that you make many mistakes. While we always recommend saving a few minutes to proofread at the end, eraser marks can make your paper messy, and big errors that require cross-outs and arrows can be confusing for graders. As much as possible, get your writing right the first time, even if that requires slowing down a bit.

We won't be going over grammar, punctuation, and usage rules in this book, but if you'd like to improve on those writing skills, you may find our book *Grammar Smart* helpful.

BEYOND MECHANICS

While you might have mastered the punctuation, grammar, and spelling rules, there are many other writing aspects that separate a mediocre essay from a top-scoring one, even if the writers have equally good ideas. Let's take a look at a few ways to take your essay from average to outstanding.

1. **Vary your sentence structure.** A paragraph that has lots of short sentences sounds choppy and simplistic. Likewise, having too many extremely long sentences can be tiring for the reader and make your point hard to understand. Try to write with a mix of short and long sentences, and vary the structure of the sentences. Here's an example of what not to do.

> *The author states that nonviolence is the best method for making social changes. He says that he wants to convert his audience through this system of civil disobedience. Gandhi uses examples to prove his argument. He also establishes trust with his audience by identifying their shared goals.*

Notice that even though the sentences don't literally start out the same, they all begin with some way of saying "the author." This makes the paragraph rather boring.

> The author states that nonviolence is the best method for making social changes. Using examples to prove his argument, Gandhi says that he wants to convert his audience through this system of civil disobedience. Furthermore, identifying their shared goals allows Gandhi to establish trust with his audience.

The same paragraph can be improved by starting the sentences in different ways. Try changing the order of the ideas within your sentence—for instance, you can start a sentence with an introductory idea that is followed by a comma. You can also try putting the author or subject later in the sentence to avoid repetition.

2. **Use creative transitions.** Most essays will have multiple examples or multiple parts of the argument. Transitions are a helpful way to move smoothly between those different components. In elementary school, you learned simple transitions such as *First*, *Then*, and *Finally*. These transitions are better than nothing, but they aren't very interesting. Try using more elaborate transitions. For instance, you could write:

> In addition to self-driving cars, smart thermostats also reveal a benefit of modern technology.

This transition ties back to the previous example (*self-driving cars*) and moves smoothly into the next (*smart thermostats*). It also references the thesis statement, which relates to the benefits of technology. Be sure to use a different kind of transition for each body paragraph after the first one to make your writing more interesting.

3. **Provide specific, detailed examples.** Some students have the impression that statements such as *Many important problems exist in the world* show that you are so knowledgeable about your topic that you do not need to provide further details. However, graders have the opposite view; broad claims without specific proof will not earn you a great score. For essays that involve making an argument, examples can be a helpful way to illustrate your point and show that you understand the real-world implications of the prompt. Where applicable, rather than

writing a vague or hypothetical example (*Sometimes two people may be having an argument...*), try to come up with a concrete example that can both show off your knowledge and give specific proof to support your point.

When you are writing about texts or images that have been provided, use specific details from those sources. This may come in the form of quoting or paraphrasing specific statements or discussing precise portions of the images. These specific details will show the grader that you carefully read or examined the provided sources, and they help prove the point you are making.

4. **Use precise language and an appropriate tone.** You may have had a teacher who instructed you never to use words such as *stuff*, *things*, or *said* in favor of using more precise language. This is good advice for any essay; wherever possible, use the most precise language. Not only do you make your intended meaning clearer, but you will also have a more interesting essay if you use more precise language. Adjectives and adverbs help too! For instance, instead of saying that an author simply *argues*, why not say that she *skillfully argues*? These additions to your sentences make your writing more interesting and, as a bonus, add length to your essay, which can help boost your score. While precise language does not always require the use of fancy vocabulary words, using more advanced vocabulary can certainly score you bonus points; just be sure that you are certain about how to use the word correctly.

    An appropriate tone is also crucial. Most essays should be written using an academic tone (email replies for foreign language exams and personal essays may be exceptions). Avoid slang and casual language (*legit*, *pretty good*, *kind of*) as well as contractions (write *it is* rather than *it's*). Don't be so focused on writing in a formal tone that you forget to make your writing interesting, however; the best essays have an academic tone but use creative transitions, precise language, and varied sentence structure to keep the reader's attention.

5. **Make it easy to read.** Most of the essays described in this book will be written by hand. This means you'll need to have neat handwriting. No shame if you are a messy writer, but when it comes to an essay test, you will simply need to slow down to write neatly. If the grader cannot read your writing, you will not receive a good score. Having clear, easy-to-read handwriting starts you off on the right foot and makes the grader's job easier. It's also a good idea to clearly indent each paragraph; you can even leave a blank line in between the paragraphs if you'd like. No grader wants to look at a full page of writing that doesn't appear to have any separation of ideas. Avoid messy erasures and cross-outs (planning ahead helps you avoid this), and don't write outside of the area you're instructed to write in. If you do need to rewrite something and it's too much to quickly erase, just put a single line through everything you want to cross out.

GIVE THE GRADERS WHAT THEY WANT

It's not enough to write an amazing essay, however. Your essay can be clear, well-written, and well-structured, but if it does not fulfill the requirements of the rubric, it will not earn a good score. In the first portion of this book, you saw a rubric for each essay on the test(s) you will be taking.

 Understanding the rubric is key to doing well on the essay: if you know what the grader is looking for, then you can focus your time on fulfilling precisely those criteria in your essay.

Some essays are scored holistically, meaning that the grader assigns you a single score based on the essay as a whole. In this case, many essay graders begin by asking themselves whether an essay is "top half" or "bottom half" in order to begin to narrow down the score. Imagine if you are a grader looking at a messy, difficult-to-read essay or one that is much shorter than usual. This essay might have some good things about it, but you are probably going to think that it is in the bottom half because longer essays tend to score better (since they have more details) and illegible essays are a pain for a grader who only has a minute or two to score each essay. Start yourself off on the right foot by having a neatly written and long essay so that the grader will begin by thinking your essay falls in the top half. Of course, a long essay filled with irrelevant details won't earn a good score, but an essay that is long because its points are fully developed will generally score higher.

Other essays are scored according to more specific components. For instance, the rubric might state that you earn a point if you cite the correct century in which an event occurred, and you won't earn the point if you omit this information or state the date incorrectly. In this case, it will be extremely helpful to be well-versed in the essay's rubric, as you will know exactly what you need to include in your essay to get full marks.

In a few cases, your essay won't be scored at all; rather it is sent to the institutions you are applying to for their review. For these tests, you'll need to understand what the admissions officers are looking for and how to make your essay stand out. You can find more details on that in the test index sections for those tests.

BRING MORE THAN JUST A PENCIL

On test day, you won't be able to bring notes into the testing center, but you can (and should!) take a mental plan for your essay or essays. Not only can you study and prepare for the specific content on your exam, but you can also plan exactly how you are going to write your essay. For instance, you should develop a template that you can use for each essay, a plan of what kinds of information will be in each paragraph. Then you just have to fill in the details with your points and arguments for whatever prompt you get on test day. In the following chapters, you'll learn how to develop a template that is appropriate for each essay you must write.

The structure of your essay isn't the only aspect that you can plan in advance. Transitions and other phrases can be prepared before test day. For instance, if you are writing an argumentative essay, you may decide that each body paragraph will have a different example. You could plan a transition for the second and third body paragraphs that you can just "fill in the blanks" for on test day. For a rhetorical analysis essay, you already know that your thesis is going to be that the author effectively accomplishes a certain goal using rhetorical techniques. You could plan how you'd like to phrase your thesis statement and simply fill in the details of the specific features of the text you are given on test day.

All of this advance planning allows you to save a lot of time on test day so that you'll be able to write plenty of details, which in turn will give you a higher score. Plus, your planned-in-advance structure, transitions, and other aspects of your essay will most likely be more effective than what you might have thrown together on test day without any preparation. Another important benefit is that you'll reduce your pre-test jitters; it can be stressful not knowing what questions or documents will be thrown at you on test day, so having everything other than the specifics of the content planned out in advance will help you to feel as confident and prepared as possible. You'll find more information on what and how to plan in advance in the other chapters of this book.

Plan as much as possible in advance to save time and reduce stress on test day.

SOME TIPS FOR COMPUTER-BASED TESTS

If the test you are taking will be done on the computer, you may have noticed that some of our advice (such as the one about having neat handwriting) does not apply. Of course, most of the strategies in this book will be applicable regardless of the format of the test. However, let's take a look at a few specific tips for essays that you will type.

1. **Learn how to type quickly.** If you tend to use the "hunt-and-peck" method of typing with one finger at a time, you'll be hurting yourself on test day, as you won't be able to get your thoughts out quickly enough. To set yourself up for success, try using typing software or even spending more time text-chatting with friends on a computer with a full keyboard (the speed of a conversation can help encourage you to type faster). Even if you are quick at typing on a phone, that won't translate directly to typing on a computer keyboard, so practice until you can do it quickly.

2. **Watch for typos.** On a paper-based test, you aren't likely to write *bit* instead of *but*, for example, but that's a common error on typed essays. Those small errors can make your essay harder to read and understand, and they give the impression of carelessness, so read over your words as you go to make sure you haven't made an error, and be sure to double check your essay for typos before the time runs out.

3. **Turn off spell check and auto-correct.** For your test, you won't have access to the tools that you might often rely on to correct any errors. For instance, you may be used to typing *youre* and having it automatically corrected to *you're*, but on test day you'll have to put in the apostrophe yourself. Get used to typing everything correctly by turning off those tools in your web browser and any word processing programs you use.

4. **Plan, but know that you'll be able to edit.** One benefit of a computer-based test is that you can go back and rewrite. On a pencil-and-paper test, you're stuck with the thesis statement you wrote in your introduction, even if you change your mind. With a computer-based test, you can always go back and change what you've written. It's still a good idea to plan in advance in order to have a more cohesive essay, especially for longer responses, but there is more flexibility. For instance, you don't necessarily have to determine your examples before you begin writing, as you could go back and fill them into the introduction later. Just don't forget to do so!

Summary:

- Prewriting is key to a smooth writing experience and a top-scoring essay. Before writing, make a plan that addresses all aspects of the prompt and has a point for each paragraph.
- Every essay needs a beginning, middle, and end. So does each paragraph.
- Use correct punctuation, grammar, and spelling to make your writing clearly understandable.
- Be specific and try to make your writing interesting while maintaining an appropriate tone.
- Know what the graders want for each essay you will be writing.
- Plan as much as you can before test day.

Next Steps:

- ❐ Get to know the rubric for your essay(s).
- ❐ Develop a plan for how you will prewrite on test day.
- ❐ For handwritten tests, practice writing neatly. For computer-based tests, work to improve your typing speed.

Chapter 5

Short Answer Approaches

Applicable to: AP Art History, AP Comparative Government and Politics, AP European History, AP U.S. History, AP World History: Modern, AP U.S. Government and Politics, AP Spanish Literature and Culture

Goals

In this chapter, you will learn how to:

- make sure you answer each part of a question
- stick to the question being asked
- organize the various types of short-answer questions

Short-answer questions ask you to do some of the same things you are required to do in a long essay but in a shorter period of time, around 5–20 minutes. This wide range of time means that the definition of "short" answer can vary significantly among different test types. In this chapter, we'll take a look at some overall short-answer strategies as well as some that will differ depending on the type of essay.

GET TO THE POINT

A short-answer response is just that—short. This means you won't have the time to fill your essay with "fluff" or craft an elaborate structure. The good news is that these essays are primarily graded on content. The scorers are looking for you to effectively answer what the question is asking, not to come up with your own ideas or make connections to the real world. Instead of a rubric, these questions have a right answer, and you'll get points so long as your answer is close enough to one of the acceptable responses. For instance, you may be asked to define a key term or to identify an artist's technique. These questions have concrete right and wrong answers, and that's what you'll be graded on.

Don't try to be creative; just answer what the question is asking based on what you have learned in your academic course.

A Plan Still Helps

Even though these essays are less elaborate, they still need a beginning, middle, and end. We recommend that you briefly jot down in the test booklet your answer to each question so that you will know what to write about and to make sure you don't miss any part of what is being asked. For example, a prompt could ask you to identify two features of a work of art, explain two techniques used in it, and compare it to an earlier art movement. Before you start writing, list several features and techniques from the work of art, and decide which two of each you'd like to write about. Then, decide which art movement you'd like to compare them to and note some main points of comparison that you will later incorporate into your answer.

If there is any part of the question you don't fully know the answer to, just try your best, as there is no harm (other than wasted time) in giving a wrong answer; you simply won't get the point, as would happen if you left the information out. Even short-answer questions may offer more than one point, so you may still be able to earn something even if you don't know the answer to part of the question.

The Answer Must Be Correct

That being said, an overly broad answer isn't likely to do you much good. The rubric specifies that you must answer the question in a particular way (or in one of a list of possible ways), and if your answer is too vague, you won't get the point.

The prompt asks for the definition of a representative democracy.

> *A representative democracy is a democracy where people are represented.*

The author of this answer may well understand what a representative democracy is, but that isn't clear from this answer. It's too vague and doesn't prove to the grader that the student fully knows the definition, so this student wouldn't earn the point for this response.

> *A representative democracy is a form of government in which people are represented by elected representatives, who are responsible for making laws. This is in contrast to a direct democracy, in which each person has a direct say in the creation of laws.*

This answer provides a much more precise definition. Even though the question did not ask about a direct democracy, by noting this distinction, the author is able to more effectively show that he or she fully understands what a representative democracy is. You won't lose points for providing extra information, as long as it does not directly contradict the correct answer, so err on the side of adding more details to prove that you know the answer to the question.

HOW TO ORGANIZE

Some short-answer questions ask you to do only one thing, such as define a term. Others contain multiple questions. These multi-part questions come in two formats: one kind is already split into multiple parts (a, b, c, etc.), and the other just asks multiple questions in a single prompt.

Pre-Split

Start by writing the letter for each part on your lined paper so that you don't miss one, and write approximately one paragraph (2 to 4 sentences) for each. Even if the question asks for something very simple (like "Identify two rights guaranteed by the First Amendment"), you should always answer in complete sentences and be as specific as possible. Remember, extra details can't hurt your score, and they may help you to earn points. It is a good idea to *explain* your answer, even if the question merely asks you to *state* your answer, as your explanation can help ensure that your response is marked correct.

Multiple Questions

When all the questions are in a single prompt, you can choose how to address each part—just make sure you don't miss any! Let's use the example from earlier, a prompt that asks you to identify two features of a work of art, explain two techniques used in it, and compare it to an earlier art movement.

In that case, you could organize your paragraphs as such:

Paragraph 1—Two features

Paragraph 2—Two techniques

Paragraph 3—Comparison to earlier movement

On the other hand, you could organize it like this:

Paragraph 1—One feature and the technique used to create it

Paragraph 2—Second feature and its technique

Paragraph 3—Comparison to earlier movement

Alternatively, here's a third option:

Paragraph 1—One feature, its technique, and how they compare to the earlier movement

Paragraph 2—Second feature, its technique, and how they compare to the earlier movement

So, you can organize in whatever way makes the most sense for the ideas you will be including. Since this type of essay will most likely contain several paragraphs, due to the multiple parts of the question, it's a good idea to plan out the focus of each paragraph in addition to jotting down your simple answers to the questions before you start writing. However, you don't need an introduction or conclusion paragraph, so focus on what the question is asking. Organization helps the grader follow the points you are making, but you are being scored here on the accuracy of your answers and explanations much more than on your writing skills, so don't spend too much time on organization.

Summary:

- Answer the question. You are primarily being graded on whether your answer is correct, not on how well-written your response is.
- Be specific and write more than the bare minimum to ensure you earn each point. You can't lose points for extra information, as long as it doesn't directly contradict the answer the graders are looking for.
- Jot down your answers before you start writing.
- Write in complete sentences. For essays with multiple paragraphs, plan the point of each paragraph before beginning the essay.

Next Steps:

☐ Learn the terms, theories, movements, events, and so on associated with the test you are taking, as they are likely to come up on the short-answer questions.

Chapter 6

Long Essay Approaches

Applicable to: All test types

Goals

In this chapter, you will learn how to:

- organize your thoughts into a clear paragraph structure
- clearly express your thesis statement for the grader
- establish the tone of your essay in an introduction
- develop each main idea in its own body paragraph
- effectively conclude your essay, whether you're pressed for time or not

WHAT'S THE PLAN?

As we've seen before, planning is a necessary part of writing an essay, especially when you are tasked with a long response. With the time pressure of the essay tasks, it may not feel like planning and outlining are a good use of time, but that time you spend coming up with a plan will set you up for success. Think of it like cooking a new dish without a recipe. It may turn out fine, but it is probably not going to be great. Having a plan for your essay gives you a framework for your ideas and will help you stay on track to finish your essay on time.

A plan is also essential in order to ensure that you are responding to all parts of the prompts. By writing an outline, you can plan where to put in the necessary number of examples, sources, or text sections that are required for a high score.

Along with the main content or analysis of your essay, you'll need a beginning and an end, or in other words, an introduction and a conclusion. Without them, you'll be dropping your reader into the middle of the action with no set-up and no resolution. We'll take a closer look at introductions and conclusions later in this chapter. For now, know that as you plan your essay, you'll need to plan for an introduction and conclusion.

THE CLASSIC 5-PARAGRAPH STRUCTURE

Chances are, at some point you've written an essay for school. And the method you were taught for doing so was like this one, the 5-paragraph essay:

1. Introduction
2. Body Paragraph 1
3. Body Paragraph 2
4. Body Paragraph 3
5. Conclusion

The 5-paragraph structure is a classic for a reason. It has a beginning, middle, and end. It gives you enough space (3 body paragraphs) to develop your argument. And it's easy to remember. Because you are familiar with this structure, it will be easy for you to replicate it during the stressful timed writing sections of the tests. We're going to dive into each part of the 5-paragraph essay structure and discuss what should be included in each paragraph. Before we do that, though, we need to talk about a very important part of your essay: the thesis statement.

AND YOUR POINT IS?

Have you ever started telling someone a story and then forgot why you were telling this particular story to this particular person? You keep talking, adding in more details, hoping that you'll remember why you started. As you talk, you can tell you're losing the interest of the other person. Eventually, you stop talking and leave both you and your listener wondering what the point of all that was.

A story without a point is like an essay without a thesis. You can have wonderful insights and detailed analyses, but without a thesis, your reader is left asking the question, *why are they telling me this?* The thesis statement is the why. Before you put pencil to paper, you need to know why you're writing this particular essay beyond the fact that it's part of a test. If you don't, your essay is going to be a loose collection of statements.

 The thesis statement is so important that it has its own grading section in many rubrics.

Coming up with a thesis statement is your first task in planning your essay. When you read a prompt, you may immediately come up with an idea. If that happens, great! You can start gathering and organizing support for your thesis. If not, don't panic. If sources or other information have been provided, read them to help find some direction, similar to how a cook might look to see what ingredients are available before determining what recipe to make. If the topic is more open-ended, do some brainstorming and jot down any ideas you have. Once you have done so, look to see if there's a common thread or theme among them. From that, you can build your thesis. If you are writing an argument essay, make sure that you pick a side in your thesis, not simply note that there are pros and cons. We'll look at a particular structure that can help you develop a thesis for argument essays in the Argumentative Essays chapter.

Defending Your Point

Once you have an idea for a thesis statement, you'll want to check to make sure it is good, by which we mean defensible. In short, be sure you're making a claim that you can back up with examples and evidence. Let's take a look at a few examples.

The prompt asks students to evaluate how innovations in science and technology affected the U.S. economy in the second half of the twentieth century.

> *Scientific and technological innovation changed the United States economy in the latter half of the twentieth century.*

This thesis statement is bad for several reasons. The first problem is that it restates the prompt. Your thesis statement should not simply restate or rephrase the prompt. The second problem is that the thesis statement doesn't address the question, which is *how*, or the extent to which, innovation changed the U.S. economy. That brings us to the third problem: this thesis statement is not an argument. No one would argue that scientific and technological innovation did not change the U.S. economy in 1950–2000. It's important that your thesis statement actually has a point!

> *Scientific and technological innovation had a greater influence on the United States economy in the years 1950–2000 than in any other period in U.S. history.*

This thesis statement is better because it makes a claim by comparing the impacts of innovation on the U.S. economy in different time periods. It doesn't include any reasoning, though, and it is rather broad. Furthermore, by claiming that this period's economy was *more* affected than that of *any other period*, the writer could easily get off track by writing about other time periods, which weren't asked about in the prompt.

> *Scientific breakthroughs in nuclear technology, data processing power, and transportation dramatically reshaped the U.S. economy in the second half of the 20th century through the creation of the military-industrial complex, Silicon Valley, and outsourced manufacturing.*

This thesis statement is more detailed and more precise than the previous ones. It does not merely restate the prompt or make broad, vague statements. It answers the prompt by saying that the innovations *dramatically reshaped the U.S. economy*, and it includes specific examples that will be developed in the body paragraphs. While it's not essential to include the examples in the thesis statement, it can help to include the reasoning that supports your stance.

Generally, thesis statements are one sentence and placed in the introduction. However, some tests will allow a thesis statement to be multiple sentences if those sentences are close together and will allow it to be placed in the introduction or conclusion or even anywhere in the essay.

 It is worth reading the rubrics of the tests you are taking to find out how long your thesis statement can be and where it can be placed.

As noted in the General Advice chapter, it's useful to come up with your own standard essay outline for the tests you are taking so you don't have to make as many decisions on test day. Consider how long you want your thesis statement to be and where you'll place it, and then be consistent.

INTRODUCTION

An introduction provides the set-up for your essay, orients the reader to what you'll be discussing, and usually contains your thesis statement. When writing an introduction, it's helpful to pretend that the reader has no familiarity or knowledge with the prompt. Write your introduction in such a way that it includes the necessary information for a reader to understand the rest of your essay.

When it comes to discussing the prompt, think about what type of essay you are being asked to write. For argument essays, pretend that you woke up with strong feelings about the topic and needed to write an essay about it. Avoid saying things like, "I agree/disagree with this statement." For essays that do ask you to respond directly to something in the prompt, like a viewpoint or text, you can include information from the prompt in your introduction.

The prompt asks students to evaluate a speech's rhetorical choices.

> *In this speech, the author makes many rhetorical choices. The eloquent speech discusses Kennedy's life and the impact he made. Ethos, pathos, and logos are some of the choices Obama made in his speech.*

This introduction has a very weak thesis. The phrase *many rhetorical choices* is vague and simplistic. Then, the author of this introduction simply mentions the rhetorical devices *ethos, pathos, and logos* without any reference to how these devices are used or how they make the text effective.

> *Presenting a eulogy at the funeral of a highly regarded individual is an honor, and in this speech, Obama eloquently displays this honor as he memorializes Ted Kennedy. Any funeral speaker would wish to illustrate the deceased's best attributes and provide a sense of pride for the family members and friends who are hearing the speech. Through the use of anecdotes, imagery, and a reverent tone, Obama elegantly achieves these goals and more.*

Rather than jumping into the specifics of the text, this introduction starts by illustrating the broader context of the speech. Showing the topic's real-world significance lets the grader know that you recognize the purpose of the given prompt. It never hurts to flatter the test-makers by suggesting that the topics and texts they have chosen are worth thinking about. This introduction also fulfills its purpose, which is to preview the rhetorical devices that will be discussed in the body paragraphs and to provide the thesis statement, which is that the author uses those devices in order to *illustrate the deceased's best attributes and provide a sense of pride.*

Generally speaking, here is what you should do in your introduction.

INTRODUCTION

1. ▶ Introduce the topic.

2. ▶ Expand on the topic with additional context or relevant information.

3. ▶ Present the thesis statement (optional).

4. ▶ Introduce examples/evidence that will be discussed in the body paragraphs.

BODY PARAGRAPHS

Body paragraphs are where your reasoning and insights are going to shine. These paragraphs give you the opportunity to provide details for each example or piece of evidence, specifically how it relates back to and supports your thesis.

When it comes to organizing your body paragraphs, you have options. Generally, each body paragraph will center on an example or a set of related examples. For instance, if you are writing a rhetorical analysis essay, each body paragraph can focus on one type of rhetorical device used in the text. For our earlier example about the effects of science and technology, each paragraph would focus on one innovation and its impacts.

Regardless of the focus of your paragraph, it should include the following:

BODY PARAGRAPHS

1. ▶ Begin with a topic sentence (and transition for 2nd and 3rd body paragraphs).

2. ▶ Explain the example/evidence.

3. ▶ Connect back to the thesis statement.

Here are some examples of body paragraphs to illustrate these points.

The prompt for this document-based question asks about the various effects of the Articles of Confederation. This student's thesis is related to political, economic, and social effects, so each body paragraph focuses on one of those areas.

The Articles of Confederation had a significant economic impact. The government did not have the power to tax the states, so it had no way of getting money, which it needed to repay debts it owed to other countries and also to pay those who fought in the war (Doc C). In 1787, Shay's Rebellion took place. 1,500 farmers in Massachusetts rebelled because they were angry about high taxes and not having enough money. They also had not been paid for their service to the country in the Revolution. Due to the Articles of Confederation, the government could only "recommend" laws to states, not enforce them, so the document was weak and ineffective politically.

This paragraph doesn't begin with a transition, which is a problem if it is a second or third body paragraph. It also does not make a strong connection between the limitations of the Articles of Confederation and the actual economic impacts that the author claims in the topic sentence. Finally, this paragraph veers off in a different direction by discussing political effects of the document, when this paragraph was supposed to focus on economic impacts.

In addition to the document's political effects, the Articles of Confederation had a significant economic impact. The government did not have the power to tax the states, so it had no way of getting money, which it needed to repay debts it owed to other countries and also to pay those who fought in the war (Doc C). In 1787, Shay's Rebellion took place. 1,500 farmers in Massachusetts rebelled because they were angry about high taxes and not having enough money. They also had not been paid for their service to the country in the Revolution. However, even though the government could not control the states, not everyone was unhappy with the arrangement. Some states benefited from the lack of trade regulations and did not want the government to be involved (Doc A). Overall, though, with a government unable to get money by means other than printing it, creating inflation, the Articles of Confederation hurt America as a whole economically.

This paragraph begins with a transition that ties back to the author's previous topic—in this case, the political effects of the Articles of Confederation. The paragraph has a clear focus on economic effects and discusses multiple, interrelated effects, and it ends with a strong statement that clearly relates to the author's thesis on the effects of the Articles of Confederation.

CONCLUSION

Your essay needs to have a conclusion, an end. Think about how frustrating it is when a TV show ends with a cliffhanger. You have all these questions and want to know what happens to your favorite characters, but the show just ends with no answers and no resolution. Your essay grader is unlikely to have as strong an emotional reaction if your essay ends without a conclusion, but there will be disappointment, and that tends to translate to a lower score.

Don't end your essay on a cliffhanger.

When to Keep It Simple

Ideally, you'll have time to write a quality conclusion. The reality, however, is that you may be running out of time. If that is the case, a simple conclusion is better than none. Restate your thesis, reiterate your reasoning, and call it a day.

When to Flesh It Out

If you have time, add more to your conclusion so that you leave the reader on the best possible terms. Use your conclusion to summarize your thesis and then leave the reader with a closing thought. A good essay takes the reader on a journey. You start somewhere familiar and walk through a series of examples and evidence that ideally helps your reader reach a new location, or, more accurately, a new way of viewing the topic.

Try to avoid broad, general statements, as the rubrics for many of the tests are specifically looking for precise language and thoughts.

Here are a few examples of conclusions.

>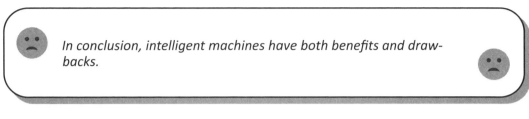
> *In conclusion, intelligent machines have both benefits and draw-backs.*

This is better than having no conclusion at all, but it's simplistic and does not specifically reference the author's thesis.

> *Overall, different types of intelligent machines have different effects. The issue of how to respond to new technology is one that we must all consider carefully.*

Again, this response is vague and doesn't directly tie back to the points the essay made earlier. It's never a bad thing to draw a connection between your topic and its relevance to our lives today, but phrases like *we can learn a lot from history* or *this is an important issue that affects everyone* are overly simplistic and don't add much to your essay. In fact, many AP Exam rubrics explicitly mention that general statements like these may prevent you from earning a top score.

> *While intelligent machines can result in improvements to our society, it will be critical for governments to respond to their rise by implementing social programs to ensure that people can not only survive but have what they need to be happy and healthy. We can all benefit from the reduction in work that technology can provide, but only if our society is thoughtful about how changes in our employment structure will be addressed.*

This conclusion sums up the author's thesis and highlights the importance of the issue at hand. It also sounds like an ending; it doesn't introduce a new topic or go off in a different direction. Let's see the general guidelines for conclusions:

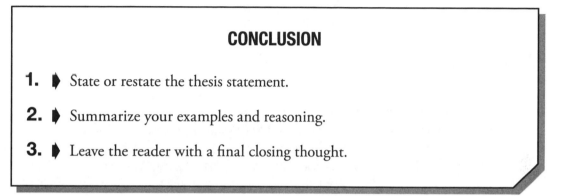

CONCLUSION

1. ▶ State or restate the thesis statement.

2. ▶ Summarize your examples and reasoning.

3. ▶ Leave the reader with a final closing thought.

You can find many more examples of solid introductions, conclusions, and body paragraphs in the example essays in the test index.

IS THERE ANOTHER WAY?

The 5-paragraph structure should not be viewed as a hard-and-fast rule. For some shorter essays, you may have only two body paragraphs, instead of three, or if you have time to fully develop a fourth point or example, you might add an additional body paragraph. Feel free to come up with your own structure that works for you and your essay. However, it's best to do that when you're practicing, in advance of test day, so that you already have a plan when the test rolls around. That way, you can focus your time on developing your ideas, not on determining your essay's structure. As we discussed in the General Advice chapter, you should have your essay template planned out in advance, whether it is the 5-paragraph structure or something else.

Summary:

- Decide on your essay structure before test day.
- Use the 5-paragraph essay template, unless you have another preference.
- Long essays generally require an introduction paragraph and a conclusion paragraph.
- Each body paragraph should have a specific focus and a beginning, middle, and end.
- Most rubrics explicitly score you on your thesis statement. Make sure you clearly state the point of your essay and make a defensible argument.

Next Steps:

- ❏ Identify what, if anything, the rubric(s) for your essay(s) say about where the thesis statement should go and how it is being scored.
- ❏ Look at example essays to see what kind of structure will be effective for each essay type.
- ❏ Decide what structure you will use for your long essay(s), and practice with it before test day.

Chapter 7

Analyzing Textual Content

Applicable to: AP European History, AP U.S. History,
AP World History: Modern,
AP U.S. Government and Politics,
AP English Language and Composition,
AP French/German/Italian/Spanish Language and Culture,
AP Latin, AP Spanish Literature and Culture, TOEFL

Goals

In this chapter, you will learn how to:

* identify important information in text-based documents
* make connections to the prompt, to your coursework, and to other documents

Some of the exam questions will provide you with documents or perspectives to use when answering the question. These can range from short-answer questions that have a single document to the six documents in the AP English Language Synthesis question and the seven documents in the Document-Based Question (DBQ) of the AP History Exams. This chapter will go over the steps to take when you are working with text-based documents.

As with all essays, it's important to have a plan. The exams do not give you much time to answer the questions, so anything you can do beforehand will help. For a more detailed look at planning and outlining, take a look at the chapters on Short Answer Approaches and Long Essay Approaches. Regardless of your essay type, you should take some time to understand the text before you begin writing. Let's take a look at our approach for how to do so.

WORKING WITH DOCUMENTS BASIC APPROACH

As you work through these steps, remember that you can circle, underline, add notes, draw arrows, or write anything else that helps you summarize and identify the key aspects of the documents.

1. **Read the prompt and/or question(s) carefully.** Make sure you know what you need to answer before you look at the documents, and underline aspects of the text that address the question. This will help you narrow in on the most relevant parts of the documents. For questions that ask you to use multiple documents, keep in mind how many documents you'll need to include in your essay.

2. **Identify relevant information.** As you read through the document(s), use SOAPS:

S = Speaker

■ Who wrote it?

◆ Are you familiar with the person?
◆ What can you infer about the author?

- For historical documents, is the speaker writing a firsthand account or a secondhand analysis? In other words, is it a primary or secondary source?

    - A primary source is a firsthand account (from someone who personally experienced the event in some way) and includes raw information. Examples of primary sources are journal entries, photos or videos, and correspondence.
    - A secondary source is an analysis or interpretation of primary sources or the event. Examples of secondary sources are textbooks, research articles, and reviews.

O = Occasion

- When was the document written?

    - If it refers to a historical event, was it written before, during, or after the event?

- What prompted the author to write the text?

A = Audience

- Who is the document addressing? What do you know about their point of view?

P = Purpose

- What is the author's reason for writing this document?

- For literature, does it fit into a certain genre?

S = Subject

- What is the content and/or focus of the document?

- What are the text's themes?

Some of this information will be provided to you in the blurb that comes before each document, so make sure to read the blurbs carefully. It may be helpful to jot down a brief note next to each document based on the information that is relevant to your prompt. For instance, if the prompt asks you to take a stance on an issue, it might help to label each document's position on the issue or a brief note of the different points it makes. That way, when you address those arguments in your essay, you'll be able to easily identify which document can be used for support.

3. **Analyze the content.** Use this step to go beyond the *what* of the document and focus on the *why*.

Speaker

- To what extent, and in what way, is the speaker credible?

- What biases may the speaker have?

  - Both primary and secondary sources can show bias by highlighting particular facts and excluding others.

Occasion

- How does the document connect to the larger historical or social context?

  - Is the document a reaction to or a catalyst for any particular events?

Audience

- What are the demographics of the audience?

- What is the relationship between the speaker and the audience?

  - Is the speaker known to the audience?
  - Why may the speaker expect the audience to agree with the point of view in the document?

Purpose

- Why is the speaker writing this document?

- Is the document more objective (like a newspaper article) or more subjective (like a persuasive speech)?

- Is the document arguing for or against an issue?

Subject

- Why does the speaker focus on the particular content of the document?

  - Is it appealing to credibility, emotion, and/or logic?

- How does the subject of the text connect to the author's purpose?

For a DBQ, you'll need to address the point of view, the audience, the historical context, and/or the author's purpose for at least three of the documents. For other types of essays, answering these questions will help you better understand the intended purpose and impact of texts. This will be especially helpful for any essay that gives you multiple documents or asks you to synthesize the given document with your coursework.

4. **Make connections.** The connections you make will depend on what the question is asking you to do.

    - **Connect to the question:** Read the question again and look at how your analysis of the document answers it. If you haven't addressed a specific question in your analysis, do it now. If the prompt asks you to write an argument, think about how each document is connected to that argument. Does it support it? Does it introduce another viewpoint or variable?

    - **Connect to your coursework:** Some questions will ask you to incorporate information from your coursework into your answer. Your analysis of the documents will help you to make those connections. Jot down any relevant outside information. For instance, a document could reference a historical event that you have studied, or a text could contain elements that are common in a certain literary movement that you have studied.

■ **Connect to other documents:** For questions that involve multiple documents, think about how they are related to each other. You may want to
group the documents based on what side of an issue they're on. This will
make it easier to organize and write your essay. You could do this by making a chart that groups the documents based on which of two or three viewpoints they take, or you could use a system of labeling each document—for
instance, put a "P" for "Pro" if it is in favor of the issue, an "A" for "Anti" if
it is against, and an "N" for "Neutral" if it is neither.

Here's an example of how to analyze a document.

1. **Read the prompt and/or question(s) carefully.**

   Source: Thomas Paine, *The American Crisis*, December 23, 1776

   *These are the times that try men's souls. The summer soldier and the
   sunshine patriot will, in this crisis, shrink from the service of their country;
   but he that stands by it now, deserves the love and thanks of man and
   woman. Tyranny, like hell, is not easily conquered; yet we have this conso-
   lation with us, that the harder the conflict, the more glorious the triumph.
   What we obtain too cheap, we esteem too lightly: it is dearness only
   that gives every thing its value. Heaven knows how to put a proper price
   upon its goods; and it would be strange indeed if so celestial an article as
   freedom should not be highly rated. Britain, with an army to enforce her
   tyranny, has declared that she has a right (not only to tax) but "to bind us
   in all cases whatsoever."*

2. **Identify relevant information.**

   Speaker   =   Thomas Paine, primary source

   Occasion   =   the American Revolutionary War

   Audience   =   the American people

   Purpose   =   argue in favor of the war

   Subject   =   the hard fight against tyranny

3. **Analyze the content.**

   Paine is writing in favor of the revolution and American independence. Specifically, he writes in a way to inspire the readers to keep fighting because "Tyranny,
   like hell, is not easily conquered." The essay was written in the early years of the
   war when people may have been faltering in their conviction because the fight
   against the British was hard.

4.   **Make connections.**

This document could be connected to any others that are also in support of the American Revolution. It would be in opposition to any that do not support the revolution.

After you analyze each document, what you'll do next depends on the type of question you are answering.

If your question includes graphs/charts, artwork, and/or images, follow the steps in the Analyzing Quantitative and Graphical Content chapter.

If your question asks you to bring in additional information from your coursework, use the advice in the Adding Outside Information chapter.

If your question asks about multiple documents, the Synthesis chapter provides strategies for combining them in your essay.

Once you are ready to outline your essay, the chapters on Short Answer Approaches and Long Essay Approaches have more information about organizing and writing your essay.

Summary:

- Follow the basic approach for analyzing textual content:
    1. Read the prompt and questions carefully.
    2. Identify relevant information using SOAPS.
    3. Analyze the content of the documents.
    4. Make connections to your coursework and other documents.
- SOAPS stands for Speaker, Occasion, Audience, Purpose, Subject.
- Plan your system for labeling the information and viewpoints in the document.

Next Steps:

- ❐ Learn the difference between primary and secondary sources if your essay will provide historical documents.
- ❐ Use sample prompts to see what types of textual content are likely to appear on the test(s) you are taking.

Chapter 8

Analyzing Quantitative and Graphical Content

Applicable to: AP Art History, AP Comparative Government and Politics, AP European History, AP U.S. History, AP World History: Modern, AP U.S. Government and Politics, AP Chinese Language and Culture, AP English Language and Composition, AP French/German/Italian/Spanish Language and Culture, AP Spanish Literature and Culture

Goals

In this chapter, you will learn how to:

- analyze charts and graphs
- analyze art images
- analyze political cartoons

This chapter will look at how to analyze graphical content, such as charts and graphs, artwork, and political images or cartoons. Depending on the AP Exams you are taking, you may have questions that focus on a single graph or image, or you may have questions that include a mix of images and documents.

Remember to read the prompt and/or questions carefully. The questions can provide useful information about the image as well as tell you what you need to look for or analyze. When you outline your response, make sure you include an answer to each part of the question. (See the chapters on Short Answer Approaches and Long Essay Approaches for more information on outlining.)

CHARTS AND GRAPHS BASIC APPROACH

1. **Identify relevant information.** As you look at the graph or chart, answer the following questions:

    - What is the title?

    - What are the labels?

    - Is there a key/legend? What does it say?

    - What are the units?

 First understanding what information is provided will help you to accurately read the chart or graph.

2. **Analyze the chart/graph.** Look for trends and relationships between the variables. Are there consistent relationships? Are there outliers or data points that stand out? This step is when you consider what the main idea or point of the chart/graph is. It may be helpful to jot down a note or use symbols to indicate what the graph is showing. For instance, you could use up or down arrows to show that a variable is increasing or decreasing, or you could write a note that summarizes the relationship in the chart.

3. **Make connections.** The connections you make will depend on what the question asks you to do.

   ■   **Connect to the question:** Read the question again, and look at the chart/graph to see how it relates to the question. Short-answer questions will generally have a few parts that will ask you to read the chart/graph and answer questions about particular points on the graph or trends you may see.

   ■   **Connect to your coursework:** Questions on charts/graphs may ask you to incorporate information you learned during your AP coursework.

   ■   **Connect to other documents:** If the chart/graph is part of a group of documents, think about how it relates to the other documents in the group. This will help you when you have to synthesize the documents. (See more about how to combine documents in the Synthesis chapter.)

Example:

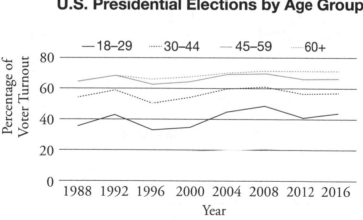

Voter Turnout Rate for U.S. Presidential Elections by Age Group

1. **Identify relevant information:**

   The graph shows the voter turnout rate for the U.S. presidential elections by age group. The vertical axis shows the percentages, and the horizontal axis shows the year, from 1988 to 2016. The key shows that the different lines are four different age groups.

2. **Analyze the chart/graph:**

    The 60+ age group has the highest voter turnout for every year. The voter turnout was higher for most groups during certain years. The 18–29 age group has the lowest voter turnout for every year.

3. **Make connections:**

    Based on information from your course and/or from any other documents that might be given, consider what affects voter turnout and how that may explain the results on the graph.

ART BASIC APPROACH

1. **Identify relevant information.** As you look at the artwork, answer the following questions:

    - Who is the artist?

    - What is the title?

    - When was it created?

    - What is the medium?

    - What is the subject matter?

    Some of this information may be provided in the prompt, or you may have to provide the answers based on your coursework.

2. **Analyze the artwork.** Think about the *how* and the *why* of the artwork. Look at how the subject matter is depicted and what that conveys to the viewer. Consider the techniques used as well as any symbols or themes present. If applicable to your course, what artistic movement is the work part of? Why was the art created? Think about the artist's motivations and where the art was originally displayed.

3. **Make connections.** The connections you make will depend on what the question asks you to do.

    - **Connect to the question:** Read the question again, and look at the artwork with the question in mind. Focus on the specific aspects that you will write about.

- **Connect to your coursework:** Use what you learned in your course to help you understand the importance of the artwork.

- **Connect to other documents:** Some questions will ask you to compare the artwork to another one you learned about in your coursework. Use your notes and analysis to help you select the artwork you will use in your comparison. (See the Synthesis chapter for tips on how to write about multiple artworks.) In other cases, a photo or other image can provide a visual for something that is described or referenced in other documents.

Example:

1. **Identify relevant information:**

   This is "The School of Athens" by Raphael, produced between 1509 and 1511. It was commissioned to depict one of the branches of knowledge: philosophy. It depicts famous philosophers in various poses.

2. **Analyze the artwork:**

An analysis of this artwork can include looking at the specific techniques Raphael used to create this piece and the artistic movement they are associated with. An analysis of the subject matter can look at the specific ways he portrays the figures, such as where they are located and what pose they are in.

3. **Make connections:**

Connections can be made between this piece and other works from around the same time that depict or focus on the ancient Greeks. You could also connect this to other works that use a similar style or those that have a similar subject matter.

POLITICAL IMAGES/CARTOONS BASIC APPROACH

Political cartoons may show up in the DBQ of the AP History Exams, and they generally provide commentary on a political issue from their time period.

1. **Identify relevant information.** As you look at the cartoon, answer the following questions:

   - Who or what is portrayed?

   - What issue or historical event is it related to?

   - Are there any people or portions of the image that are labeled? Can you identify any that are not labeled?

2. **Analyze the cartoon.** Once you identify what the cartoon is showing, think about the stance or viewpoint of the cartoonist. Is the cartoon depicting something in a positive or negative light? Does it support or oppose an issue?

3. **Make connections.** The connections you make will depend on what the question asks you to do.

   - **Connect to your coursework:** Think about how the cartoon connects to the historical event or issue you covered in your coursework.

   - **Connect to other documents:** How does the cartoon connect to other documents in the group? Which documents take the same stance as the cartoon?

Example:

1. **Identify relevant information:**

   The cartoon shows a man and woman. The first three panels show him trusting her with money, the household, and the children. In the fourth panel, the woman asks why she can't be trusted with the ballot. This cartoon is about women's suffrage.

2. **Analyze the cartoon:**

   This cartoon is in support of women's suffrage. By showing the other things that women are trusted with (money, homes, children), it makes the case that women should also be trusted with the right to vote. The woman looks exhausted in the third panel, which could further imply that the artist believes women are burdened by many household tasks but not compensated with access to a basic right.

3. **Make connections:**

   This cartoon could connect to any other documents that are supportive of women's suffrage. It provides a logical reason women should be eligible to vote that is related to trust.

Summary:

- Follow the basic approach.
  1. Identify relevant information.
  2. Analyze the content.
  3. Make connections.
- Make notes regarding the graphs or images in order to formulate your thesis and support.

Next Steps:

- ❏ Use sample prompts to determine what kinds of graphs or images may appear on the test(s) you are taking.
- ❏ If you tend to struggle with understanding graphs or identifying features on images, practice with sample prompts before test day.

Chapter 9

Combining Outside Information and Given Information

Applicable to: AP European History, AP U.S. History, AP World History: Modern, AP English Language and Composition

Goals

In this chapter, you will learn how to:

- give context for provided documents
- add evidence beyond the provided documents

Although you are given documents for the Document-Based Question and the English Synthesis essay, you'll need to go beyond the given information to write a good essay. The readers will be looking for you to expand upon the content of the documents by bringing in your outside knowledge, either from your coursework or from your own brainstorming on the topic. This chapter will go over how to bring in outside information.

NARRATION VS. ANALYSIS

One of the most important things to keep in mind while working on these essays is that you must do more than summarize the given documents.

> Your goal is not to show off your ability to read and understand the documents; your goal is to write an essay with a clear point of view that is supported and/or complicated by the given documents.

Although you do want to make sure to represent the documents correctly, it is not enough to describe them (see the chapters on analyzing content for ways to work with the documents). Low-scoring essays are ones in which students summarize all of the documents without relating them to an overall argument. For every document, you need to ask yourself how it connects to your thesis. This is where bringing in outside information can help you. Adding context to the documents will demonstrate the skills and knowledge you've learned in your courses as well as help you to connect the documents to the overall argument of your essay.

CONTEXT MATTERS

What type of context you can provide for a document will vary based on your familiarity with the document and the topic it focuses on. Here are some different ways you can add context to show what you know.

Providing Definitions

Outside information can include defining terms or explaining references within the document. For instance, if one of the documents mentions the Stamp Act, you could explain what that policy entailed. If you are given a political cartoon that references the Three Little Pigs, you could briefly note who those characters are. Such details make your essay more complete and help the reader understand the points you are making.

Giving Historical Context

You may also think about the historical, political, and/or social context. This is especially true for the AP History Exams, as you have all of the course content to draw on. For example, if you are told what year a document was written, you could describe other events that had recently occurred to further explain the information in that document.

Analyzing Perspectives

Point of view can also lend itself to adding outside knowledge. You can consider who the author is and what stance the document takes. If you are familiar with the author, or even if you know the author's job or background, you can use that information to go beyond the content of the document and discuss the author's point of view and purpose. For example, if the document were written by a farmer, you could draw a connection between what is stated in the text and what you know about events that would have affected the farmer's point of view.

Identifying the Audience

Another aspect to consider is the audience: the general population, a specific group of people like lawmakers or scientists, or an individual. For instance, if the document were written for members of an army during a war, it could have been intended to boost morale and could therefore represent an overly optimistic view of the nation's circumstances. Rather than taking the statements in the document at face value, try to consider who the author and audience are, as they affect which information the document focuses on and how it approaches that information.

For the AP English essay, you can connect the documents to real-world examples, like current events or political/social issues. The outside information is not meant to stand alone; instead, outside information will assist you in analyzing the documents and relating them to the argument that you are making. Unlike with the history exams, you aren't expected to have specific outside knowledge on the AP English Synthesis essay topic, but it's great if you can connect the topic to everyday issues.

AP HISTORY EXAMS: CONTEXTUALIZATION AND EVIDENCE BEYOND THE DOCUMENTS

There are two parts of the AP History Exams' rubrics that specifically address adding in outside information: Contextualization and Evidence Beyond the Documents. For Contextualization, you'll need to provide a broader historical context for the prompt. This broader historical context, as the name implies, can be a sweeping change or major historical event that occurred before or during the time period in the prompt. For Evidence Beyond the Documents, you'll want to give a more specific piece of evidence that supports your argument. You can use a specific historical event, figure, law, or document that supports the point you are trying to make but is not directly discussed in the provided documents.

CONNECTING THE DOTS

Your goal is to use the given information and the added outside information to support your thesis. Your thesis statement must go beyond the points of view presented in the documents; it's not enough to use one of the points of view in the documents (see the Argumentative Essays chapter for more information on crafting a thesis). For documents that support your thesis, provide outside information that gives the author and perspective more credibility. For documents that do not support your thesis, use outside information to explain why the documents are not as strong as the ones that do support your thesis. You can do this by looking at any of the outside information discussed above. You may question the author's credibility, the author's point of view, or the way the document portrays a specific historical event or person. You can also discuss what the author fails to take into account. Your thesis and reasoning are the stars of the show; the documents and outside information play the supporting roles.

CITATIONS

Whenever you are referring to information in one of the documents, whether it's a direct quote, a reference, or a paraphrase, cite that document. The citations on the AP Exams are straightforward. For history, use Doc and the relevant number (Doc 1). For English, you can use Source and the relevant letter (Source A) or the names in the parentheses that are given in the prompt. You don't need to use a citation for your outside knowledge. Remember, however, that each paragraph should be centered around your own argument. Citations tell where you got the information, but they shouldn't be the focus of your sentence.

Here's an example.

This prompt asked about the transformative effect the 16th-century Portuguese had on maritime trade in the Indian Ocean.

According to Doc 6, "Cochin is the most important base the Portuguese have in southwestern India."

Almost the whole sentence is a quotation, so this doesn't show the grader that you know anything related to the topic.

Cochin was a very important Indian trading base for the Portuguese (Doc 6).

This can work, but only if you follow this sentence with your own analysis. Otherwise, it only shows that you can literally read the text, which isn't enough.

The Portuguese imported pepper from Cochin, an important trading base in southwestern India, but they were said to receive an inferior version (Doc 6), which illustrates the limits of the Portuguese traders' influence. Their brokers rebelled against the Portuguese by refusing to furnish them with quality products, a result of their loyalty to their own empires.

This example cites a document, but the sentences are focused around the essay-writer's point. There is a clear connection to the thesis as well as additional context.

Use the information in the documents to support your thesis.

Summary:

- It's not enough to write about the content of each document; you must analyze the documents and incorporate outside information to help with the analysis.
- Outside information helps to contextualize the documents and connect the documents to your thesis.
- For history exams, you can use any relevant content from the AP courses.
- For the English exam, you can use any relevant real-world examples.
- Make sure to use citations for any quote, reference, or paraphrase of the documents.

Next Steps:

- ☐ For history exams, learn major events and their effects so that you can connect them to what you see in the documents on test day.
- ☐ For the English exam, make a habit of reading or watching news media, as your knowledge of current events will help you to make strong real-world connections in your essay.

Chapter 10

Adding Outside Content

Applicable to: AP Art History, AP Comparative Government and Politics, AP European History, AP U.S. History, AP World History: Modern, AP U.S. Government and Politics, AP English Language and Composition, AP English Literature and Composition, TOEFL, ACT, ISEE, SSAT

Goals

In this chapter, you will learn how to:

- choose the most appropriate examples for open-ended essays
- add examples to content-based essays
- prepare examples in advance, where possible

Some standardized essays will ask you to include your own examples. Depending on the specific test, the examples you may use can range from anything you come up with to particular content covered in an AP course. This chapter will explore adding outside content to your essays, from brainstorming and selecting examples to writing those examples into your essay.

OPEN-ENDED ESSAYS

Some essays, such as the ones on the AP English Language and Composition, TOEFL, ACT, SSAT, and ISEE exams, are completely open-ended. For instance, they may ask you to come up with a specific example that fulfills a certain criterion (example: *Identify something that is more valuable than people think.*) or ask a broad question that could be supported with examples from any number of sources (example: *Should people travel the world or explore their own communities?*). Essays that allow you to include examples from any source can elicit feelings of both freedom and fear. Just because you can write about literally anything doesn't mean you should.

To maximize your chances of getting a good essay score, carefully consider what type of examples you choose.

The Seneca Falls Convention

Milgram's experiments on obedience

Okonkwo's exile in the book Things Fall Apart

The treatment of the Uyghur ethnic group within China

Anything academic is going to be a good example. Historical figures and events, literary works, and research studies are all good. You can also use current political and social events and figures. Be as specific as possible in your examples, as those details make you sound like an expert.

> *A school trip I took*
>
> *People tend to do what an authority figure tells them to*
>
> *War in general*

If you are struggling to come up with enough relevant academic or current event examples, you can use broad, personal, and/or hypothetical examples. While these should not be your first choice, they can be used in your essay. Just make sure that not all of your examples come from this category, or your essay will likely be too vague to earn a top score. Ideally, however, use the broad or hypothetical example that you think of to spur a more specific example. For instance, if you come up with *war in general* as an appropriate example, consider whether there is a specific battle or event that you can write about.

> If your essay prompt asks you about yourself, personal examples are completely valid. See the chapter on Personal Essays for more on that.

> *The TV show <u>The Office</u>*
>
> *The video game <u>Fortnite</u>*
>
> *The Harry Potter book series*
>
> *A popular social media star*

Avoid using examples that are "low brow" in nature. Examples from pop culture, young adult literature, sports, and social media are not going to be considered as relevant or convincing as the previously stated examples. These topics can work if you can find the depth and nuance in them, but in our experience, they usually come off as shallow, and using a less academic topic takes away your opportunity to show off what you have learned in school. According to many rubrics, top-scoring essays are "sophisticated," and it's challenging to write a sophisticated essay on a topic that is viewed as shallow.

Since these essays are open-ended, it can be difficult, but not impossible, to prepare.

PREPARING FOR EXAMPLES

1. ▶ **Brainstorm in advance**. Make a list of possible specific, sophisticated examples that you can use. Write down any historical figures and events, literary works, research studies, and current events that you know well enough to write about in a body paragraph of an essay. The list may not be very long, and that's okay! Although you won't be able to access this list during the test, you can mentally run through it after reading the prompt and decide if any of your examples could work for that particular prompt. Having a list of examples may ease some of the anxiety around this part of the essay process. Of course, you can also spend some time before test day researching and memorizing key details of those examples if you need to.

2. ▶ **Practice brainstorming.** Another way to prepare is to practice brainstorming. Most tests have practice prompts that you can view online. Set a timer for a few minutes and come up with as many relevant examples as you can. As you practice, you'll find that you're able to come up with examples for a wide variety of prompts and that you can often reuse the same ones that you know well.

What If I Can't Think of Anything?

Some students worry that they'll be unable to come up with any examples when they are given a prompt on test day. The above suggestions should go a long way toward reducing any test anxiety you have around this topic. However, if you do freeze, there are some things to keep in mind.

For argumentative essays: As discussed in the Argumentative Essays chapter, you do not need to write an argument that you believe in. If you have picked your thesis statement but cannot come up with any examples to support it, it's time to brainstorm examples for other sides of the argument. As you practice these essays, if you find that you are often struggling to connect your thesis to relevant examples, then it may be worthwhile to focus on brainstorming examples first. Then you can write a thesis statement based on the examples you come up with. This will ensure that you can support and defend your thesis, which is the main thing that the graders are looking for.

For open-ended essays: For essays that give you an open-ended question, remember that you are not being scored on what you actually believe. Focus on brainstorming examples and then craft your thesis statement based on those examples. If you do have a list of prepared examples, see if you can use one of those. Even if it's not a perfect fit, a pretty good example is better than no example at all.

It's important to remember that these essays are timed. You don't want to waste time coming up with the "perfect" examples; you're being scored on your ability to defend your thesis, so your time will be better spent connecting your examples to your thesis.

CONTENT-BASED ESSAYS

For essay questions that are focused more on coursework, such as the AP Exams in art history, English, history, and government, your examples will come from the content that you studied. There are two criteria to consider when you are choosing your examples:

1. ▶ How well does the example fit the prompt? You'll want to choose examples that fit the basic constraints (a particular time period or a particular style of government, for instance), but beyond that, you have some flexibility.

2. ▶ How well can you write about the example? Assess your own knowledge of the examples you choose. You don't need to remember every detail about the example, but you need to feel comfortable writing enough to convey how the example supports your thesis.

Ideally, you'll have examples that score high on both points: they fit the prompt perfectly, and you are confident in your ability to write about them. Realistically, though, you'll probably have examples that range from okay to great. You want to pick examples that are "good enough." They fit the constraints of the prompt and address the main question, and you can write enough about them that they help defend your thesis. If any of your examples don't fit the prompt or you can't write more than a sentence about them, then you'll need to brainstorm some more. Time is a factor, so if you are running out of it, pick the best examples you have and try to make them work.

That being said, you have a good sense of what you'll see on the essay questions because they are based on your coursework. This means that you can prepare.

As part of your study plan for the exam, come up with a variety of examples that you could include in your essay.

This will look different for each test, but for instance, prepare a potential example or two for each time period or each art movement that may be tested. You may be able to use the information about the test from the College Board to determine which specific time periods, movements, or countries you will be assessed on (or be able to choose from) for your essay prompt, so use those guidelines to prepare some versatile examples that can be applied to different questions. When you have a list compiled, test it out. Look up previous exam prompts and see whether you can use any of the examples on your list to answer the question. If you find any questions that you can't answer with an example from your list, look through your coursework to find a relevant example and spend some time studying it so you can add it to your example list.

For the AP Art History and AP English Exams, the essay questions will give you a list of example works that you can write about. You do not need to use one of the listed examples, but it should preferably be one that you studied in your course. Remember to consider how well you can write about the example. If you feel knowledgeable about and comfortable with one of the listed examples, use it. If you'd rather use another example, that's fine as well. The graders are looking at how well you can answer the prompt with an example; while your example needs to be relevant to the prompt, you will not get a higher score by using one of the given examples. As with the history exams, make sure that before test day you are well-versed in several versatile artworks or books that you have studied or read during your course. This way, you'll be able to use an example that you are very familiar with regardless of what the question asks, which will allow you to write specific details and ultimately score higher.

INCORPORATING EXAMPLES

Selecting appropriate and relevant examples is only one aspect of answering these essay questions. You'll also need to be able to write the examples into your essay in a way that supports your thesis and demonstrates your knowledge. When adding your examples, include enough detail for the reader to understand your example but not so much detail that it overwhelms your essay.

This open-ended essay prompt asks you to write about something you consider to be "overrated." You may write an essay about how money is overrated, and you choose __The Great Gatsby__ as one of your examples. When writing about __The Great Gatsby__, you'll need to include enough plot and character details to establish why __The Great Gatsby__ supports your argument that money is overrated.

Jay Gatsby's death at the end of __The Great Gatsby__ shows that money can't give you everything you want.

This sentence does not include enough information. All we know is that the character dies at the end of the book. If you haven't read *The Great Gatsby*, then you have no idea how this character's death relates to the thesis.

__The Great Gatsby__, a 1925 novel by F. Scott Fitzgerald, is narrated by Nick Carraway. Carraway befriends Jay Gatsby, a man known for throwing lavish parties. Gatsby is in love with Daisy Buchanan, who is married and lives across the bay from Gatsby's mansion. Throughout the novel, Carraway becomes enmeshed with Gatsby's attempts to rekindle his romance with Daisy and convince her to leave her husband, Tom. Although Gatsby and Daisy reconnect, she ultimately chooses to stay with Tom. While driving with Gatsby, Daisy hits and kills a woman, Myrtle Wilson. Myrtle's husband thinks it was Gatsby's fault and kills him.

This is too much information for your essay. Remember that you are not writing a book report, or any other kind of report. Your examples are there to help support your thesis. Even for the tests that ask you to focus on one example, like the AP English Literature exam, your task is not to present information. Rather, your goal is to connect your examples to the point you are making.

> *In The Great Gatsby, Jay Gatsby believes he can win back the love of his life, Daisy Buchanan, by becoming wealthy. He becomes rich and ends up living in a mansion across the bay from Daisy's and throws lavish parties to get her attention. Despite all his efforts, he is heartbroken when Daisy ultimately decides to stay with her husband.*

This gives enough relevant information to understand how the novel connects to the argument. It shows that money couldn't give Gatsby what he wanted, which supports the idea that money is overrated. However, it does not make a direct connection to the author's thesis, which is an important part of each body paragraph.

In order to make certain that the connection between your thesis and your example is clear, make sure to include a sentence before your example to set it up and a sentence after your example to connect back to the thesis.

> *Although money can buy many material goods, when it comes to matters of the heart, money can't buy love. In The Great Gatsby, Jay Gatsby believes he can win back the love of his life, Daisy Buchanan, by becoming wealthy. He becomes rich and ends up living in a mansion across the bay from Daisy's and throws lavish parties to get her attention. Despite all his efforts, he is heartbroken when Daisy ultimately decides to stay with her husband. When it comes to the fundamental human need for love, Gatsby's failure shows that money isn't everything.*

By adding sentences before and after your example, you can show the readers how your example supports your thesis. This demonstrates your reasoning ability and will earn you a higher score.

For some types of essays, it's certain that the graders are familiar with your examples. However, you should still provide background information as though they aren't; this sets up your argument and shows that you understand the topic you're writing about. Just be sure that you only include enough details to support the claims you are making. Try to find a balance between showing off your knowledge on a topic and having a clear point within your body paragraph.

Summary:

- When choosing examples, consider:
  - How well does the example fit the prompt?
  - How can you write about the example?
- Good examples are academic in nature and could include historical figures and events, literary works, research studies, or current events.
- Personal, broad, and hypothetical examples can be used for open-ended essay questions, though they aren't preferred.
- Avoid examples that are "low brow," like those from pop culture.
- Brainstorm a list of possible examples, and practice using them on sample prompts.
- For essays that will test you on books, historical periods, artworks, or other materials/topics that you have studied in your course, be sure that you prepare in advance a few versatile examples that you are highly knowledgeable about.
- When adding an example to your essay, make sure to include enough relevant information to support your thesis, but don't get carried away with unnecessary details.

Next Steps:

- ❐ Make a list of possible examples that are appropriate and that you know well enough to write about in detail.
- ❐ Use sample prompts to see how your prepared examples will work and to practice brainstorming.

Chapter 11

Rhetorical Analysis

Applicable to: AP English Language and Composition,
AP English Literature and Composition,
AP Spanish Literature and Composition

Goals

In this chapter, you will learn how to:

- write an effective thesis statement for a rhetorical analysis essay
- make connections between SOAPS and rhetorical features to identify why the author made certain choices
- use quotes and paraphrase from the text to provide evidence for your claims

Rhetorical and literary analysis essays give you an opportunity to showcase your ability to understand how an author or speaker skillfully communicates a message or idea. Your goal when writing this type of essay is to analyze how the author fulfills his or her purpose. For most literary analysis prompts and some rhetorical analysis prompts, you'll be told what the author is trying to do, such as illustrate the complex relationship between two characters or convince a group of people to take a specific action. If the goal is not stated, you'll need to identify what the author is trying to do. With the author's purpose in mind, you'll next work on analyzing how the author is fulfilling his or her purpose through the use of rhetorical and literary devices. Through your studies, you've learned the different tools authors use in their writings, so this chapter will focus on how to organize and write about those tools.

RHETORICAL/LITERARY ANALYSIS ESSAY GOALS

1. ▶ Identify the author's purpose.
2. ▶ Analyze how the author's use of rhetorical devices supports his/her purpose.

THIS ISN'T ABOUT YOU

One thing to keep in mind is that this type of essay is not the place to insert your own opinions or critiques. Your task is not to criticize the author's writing or suggest ways it could have been improved. Additionally, do not write about whether or not you agree with the author because that is not the purpose of these essays.

I think that Porter could have used more imagery and better metaphors to convey the reaction Miranda has to her two older relatives.

I disagree with Gandhi's argument about the British monopoly on and taxation of salt in India in the 1930s.

The texts selected for these essays are written by authors who are good at using rhetorical devices for a specific purpose. You can safely assume that the authors are fulfilling their goals, so your job is to figure out and explain how they accomplish that goal.

 Do not critique the writing or state whether you agree or disagree with the argument.

FLATTERY WILL GET YOU EVERYWHERE

As mentioned above, the test-makers take great care in selecting well-written or well-argued pieces. With this in mind, one thing that you can do in your writing is to flatter the test-makers by pointing out how well the authors are fulfilling their goals. You can easily do this by adding in adjectives and adverbs that convey this point: "skillfully," "aptly," "deftly," "eloquent," "articulate," for example.

> *Gandhi is somewhat convincing in his protest against the British.*

Remember, never disparage the author or text.

> *Gandhi protests the British by using the rhetorical devices of diction, tone, and deductive reasoning.*

This is better, but it misses the opportunity to point out how effective the author is in achieving this goal.

> *Gandhi skillfully argues against the British monopoly on and taxation of salt though diction, a respectful tone, and articulate deductive reasoning.*

This statement praises the author, which demonstrates that the essay will show not only what the author does but also how those techniques *effectively* fulfill the author's purpose.

WHAT THE WHAT

Before diving into the rhetorical choices and their impacts (the how and the why), it's helpful to take a moment to consider the what; specifically, the author/speaker and the context. This step can also help you craft a solid introduction to your essay. To find the what, use SOAPS. (While all parts of SOAPS are applicable to the rhetorical analysis essay, some parts may be more or less useful for literary and poetry analysis. Take what works and leave the rest.)

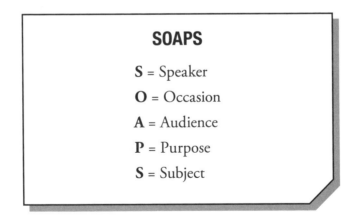

SOAPS

S = Speaker

O = Occasion

A = Audience

P = Purpose

S = Subject

S = Speaker

Who is speaking or writing?

You can think about the speaker's relationship to the material as well as to the audience. You can also consider the author's qualifications for speaking on the particular subject matter. For literary pieces, you may be familiar with the author and can use that knowledge to comment on the themes of their work or their place in the literary canon.

O = Occasion

What prompted this speech/text? What is the historical context?

For the rhetorical analysis essay, you'll generally be given the context of the speech or text in the prompt. If you are familiar with the particular historical context, you can expand upon it in your introduction. For the literary/poetry analysis, historical context will be less of a factor. However, if you are aware of any particular literary movement that the text/poem belongs to, you can include that in your introduction.

A = Audience

Who is the intended audience? What is the audience's relationship to the speaker?

Most of the rhetorical analysis texts are speeches or arguments directed at someone. As you think about the rhetorical choices that the speaker/author makes, it's helpful to think about who the recipient is. A eulogy delivered to friends and family will be very different from a speech delivered to a colonizing government. For literary analysis, it may be helpful to consider how literary devices that use the audience's outside knowledge are effective. Devices like allusions and symbols may be more effective for certain groups of people.

P = Purpose

What is the author's/speaker's intention?

As mentioned above, most of the prompts will give you the purpose. The purpose may be to persuade someone to act or to portray a complex character. The purpose will inform your analysis of rhetorical and literary devices, which we'll discuss further below.

S = Subject

What is the main idea? What are the main lines of reasoning?

The subject is the content of the piece. If the author's purpose is to examine the complexity of a relationship between a mother and daughter, the subject may be a specific event that occurs between them. If a speaker's purpose is to convince the government to stop a harmful action, the subject may be the specific ways that people are being harmed.

Identifying the parts of SOAPS should not take up much of your time. Most of the information will be in the prompt itself. When writing your essay, you'll want to put SOAPS in the introduction; this will allow you to establish the context for the rest of your essay. And, as mentioned before, the Purpose part of SOAPS will be essential in the next step of your analysis.

> *Obama gave a speech about Ted Kennedy.*

This sentence does not give any specifics about the speech besides the speaker and the subject. It's not clear why the speech was given.

> *Obama delivered a eulogy at Ted Kennedy's funeral.*

This statement is more specific, but adding more detail will allow you to make a stronger connection between what the author does and why those techniques are effective on that audience, at that time, for that purpose.

> *Senator Ted Kennedy passed away in 2009 after serving in the Senate since 1962. Former President Obama, who worked with him for several years, delivered a eulogy to praise and memorialize Senator Kennedy.*

These sentences introduce more than the previous examples do. This one sets up the relationship between the speaker and the subject, and it mentions the purpose. Notice that this example includes multiple sentences. Depending on how much context you are given or know, you may write one or two sentences summing up the SOAPS.

After introducing the SOAPS material, you can move into your thesis statement. Luckily, the thesis statement for this essay is extremely simple. Your point will be the same every time—the author effectively achieves some goal by using certain methods that you will name. We'll talk more about that and the other parts of your essay that you can prepare in advance later on in this chapter. First, let's see some of the rhetorical devices and techniques that you might notice in the text you are given.

THIS IS WHAT WE'RE LOOKING FOR

Ethos: Appeal to credibility or why the author/speaker has the knowledge/expertise to speak on the issue

>*Ex.: An epidemiologist using her credentials to convince people she has the authority to speak about infectious diseases*

Pathos: Appeal to emotion or using words or images that evoke an emotional reaction

>*Ex.: An animal shelter using photos of sad dogs and cats to raise money or showing pictures of empty cages to create a sense of joy that all animals were adopted*

Logos: Appeal to logic or using reasoning as a persuasive tool

>*Ex.: Telling people that voting for a particular bill will positively affect them*

Imagery: Using descriptive language that appeals to the senses

>*Ex.: Describing the specific taste of a food or detailing what a place looks like*

Allusion: A brief reference to something culturally significant

>*Ex.: Calling someone who betrays you "Benedict Arnold"*

Tone: Attitude of the author/speaker to the subject

>*Ex.: Using words like "suggest" and "probably" convey that the author is unsure or cautious*

Syntax: Structure of lines/sentences

>*Ex.: Using long, detailed sentences to immerse the reader in the imagery or short, choppy sentences to quicken the pace.*

Diction: Word choice

>*Ex.: Using harder vocabulary words to make a piece of writing sound more formal*

Metaphors/Similes: Comparing two distinct things; similes usually use "like" or "as"

Ex.: "The cat looked like a cloud."

Juxtaposition: Putting two opposing things next to each other to invite a comparison

Ex.: "It was the best of times. It was the worst of times."

Repetition: Repeating words or phrases for emphasis

Ex.: Martin Luther King Jr. repeated "I have a dream" in his famous speech

Hyperbole: Exaggerating

Ex.: "I'm so tired I could sleep for a week."

Statistics/Quotes: Using facts or expertise to add credibility to an argument

Ex.: "80% of people support this amendment."

Meter: The pattern of syllables and emphasis in a line of poetry

Ex.: A certain meter could mimic the beat of a waltz and make the poem feel like a dance

Rhyme Scheme: The pattern of rhymes within a poem

Ex.: An author may use a particular rhyme scheme to construct a specific type of poem, such as a sonnet

These are just a few of the many literary devices that could appear in a given text. You have probably learned many more in school. Consult your course materials for more literary devices that you can learn for test day. That being said, the AP scorers are grading you on your ability to explain how the rhetorical choices help the text achieve its goal much more so than on your knowledge of a bunch of obscure terms.

QUALITY CONTROL

As you read through the text, you can mark as many rhetorical and literary devices as you notice. You may find that some authors/speakers use a wide variety of devices, while others focus on a handful. For your essay, you'll only need 3 or 4. Once you've marked up the text, you'll need to go through and select the ones that you'll write about. Avoid the temptation of including everything you find. The graders are not looking for you to identify everything in the text; instead, they are interested in how well you can analyze the devices. In order to have enough time and space to do a thorough analysis, you need to be selective about what you'll include in your essay. Focus on the devices that are important and prevalent. Remember that you'll be writing about how the devices support the author's purpose. If you can't come up with the reason during your initial analysis, you don't want to include that particular device.

As you're choosing the rhetorical devices that you'll write about, keep in mind that there are no "right" or "wrong" devices to write about. Two top-scoring essays could focus on entirely different aspects of the text. The graders are looking at how you analyze what the authors and speakers are doing. You don't need to worry about which rhetorical devices are better to write about; instead, focus on which ones you can write about in a compelling way.

When you are organizing your essay, you can plan to discuss one rhetorical or literary device in each body paragraph. Aim for three body paragraphs, but, if you have the time, you can include an additional body paragraph. It's also possible to spend more than one paragraph on a single device if it is used in different ways. For instance, you could show how the text uses an appeal to guilt in one portion of the text and an appeal to pride in another portion of the text. Even though those both represent pathos, your descriptions will be different since the specific emotions the text evokes are different.

RHETORICAL ANALYSIS STEPS

1. ▶ Read the text and mark any literary/rhetorical devices.

2. ▶ Choose 3 or 4 devices to write about.

3. ▶ Focus on the devices that are important and prevalent.

4. ▶ Write about one device per body paragraph.

En Español

For the AP Spanish Literature and Composition Exam, make sure that you know these terms, or at least how to describe them, in Spanish.

WE'VE BEEN HERE BEFORE

As with other essay types, having a plan before test day is going to save you time and reduce your stress. Although you may not know the specifics of the texts beforehand, you do know the task. This enables you to craft templates for your thesis statement and the topic sentences of your body paragraphs. Here are a few simple templates that you can use or modify in whatever way makes sense to you.

Thesis statement templates:

(The author) effectively (purpose) by using (device 1), (device 2), and (device 3).

Through the use of (device 1), (device 2), and (device 3), (the author) skillfully argues that (their argument).

Body paragraph topic sentences:

A second way (author) adeptly (purpose) is with his/her use of (rhetorical device).

In addition to (previous device), (author) also skillfully (next device) in order to (purpose).

Come up with your own template for your thesis statement and transitions, and use that template every time you write a practice essay for the test you are taking. That way it will be automatic on test day. You can also plan out the basic structure of your introduction and conclusion, since you already have a good idea of what kinds of information need to be included there.

QUOTATIONS ARE NECESSARY; CITATIONS ARE WELCOME

Every rhetorical or literary device that you include in your essay should include a quote. It could be a single word, a phrase, or a whole sentence. No matter the length, it's essential that you use the words from the text to support your analysis. Try to avoid using large sections or multiple sentences from the text, as this can take up too much time and space. The graders are not interested in rereading the source text; they want to know your thoughts and analysis.

Poe uses words that make people think of heaven and hell, and those words help describe the love between the narrator and Annabel Lee.

This sentence doesn't quote anything directly, so there is no support for the analysis that may follow.

> 😐 Poe characterizes the love between the narrator and Annabel Lee as eternal by saying, "And neither the angels in heaven above/Nor the demons down under the sea/Can ever dissever my soul from the soul/ Of the beautiful Annabel Lee." 😐

This sentence uses a direct quote, which gives support for the later analysis. However, the quote is long, and it's not entirely clear which specific parts are relevant.

> 😄 Poe mentions "the angels in heaven above" and "the demons down under the sea," two extreme examples, to emphasize the strength of connection between the narrator and Annabel Lee. 😄

This sentence quotes the poem, but the majority of the sentence is not the quote itself. Instead, the quotes are there to support the reasoning. Never make an entire sentence out of a quote. Each sentence should be your own point; the quotation is there only to provide evidence for that point you are making.

Citations are not necessary, but you can include them. Since the test is giving you the source text, there is no possible confusion about where you are quoting from. However, if you are quoting a single word that occurs multiple times, and you want to focus on a specific instance, it can be useful to include a citation so that the graders know exactly what area you are analyzing. Citation format is not standardized for these tests, so you can use the name of the speaker/author and general area (Obama, paragraph 4) or the line number (line 6).

COMMENTARY

Identifying the rhetorical and literary devices is not enough to get a good score. In order to successfully analyze the text, you'll need to be able to explain why the author/speaker uses those specific devices and how they help fulfill the author's/speaker's purpose. You'll want to avoid simply stating the rhetorical device or quoting the text. Instead, focus on the why and the how: why did the author choose to use this device and how does it help them fulfill their purpose?

COMMENTARY GOALS

1. ❭ Why did the author/speaker use this particular rhetorical device?

2. ❭ How does this particular rhetorical device contribute to the author's/speaker's purpose?

Obama includes anecdotes about Kennedy, like this one: "When they tossed him off a boat because he didn't know what a jib was, six-year-old Teddy got back in and learned to sail." This anecdote helps Obama to memorialize Kennedy.

This example includes a rhetorical device—an anecdote—and a quote supporting that rhetorical device, but it doesn't tell us why Obama included this example or how it helps to memorialize Kennedy.

Obama includes multiple anecdotes, like one about Kennedy's family tossing him off the boat, and says that "six-year-old Teddy got back in and learned to sail." This anecdote from Teddy's childhood provides a different view from the one most people have of Ted Kennedy as a senator, which allows people to relate to him more. By discussing personal stories from Kennedy's childhood, Obama is able to memorialize Kennedy as someone who was tenacious.

This example includes the same anecdote as before, but it also includes why Obama might have included it and how it helped Obama memorialize Ted Kennedy. However, to earn a top score, more detail is needed.

> *Obama includes multiple anecdotes from Kennedy's life, like one when a six-year-old Teddy was tossed off his family's boat for not knowing a jib. Obama says that Teddy "got back in and learned to sail." This personal anecdote portrays Kennedy as tenacious, a theme that Obama expands upon later when he discusses other hardships that Kennedy faced, like multiple deaths in his family. Obama says it would have been understandable if Kennedy re-treated from public life, but instead Kennedy continued to serve as senator until his death. By discussing Kennedy's childhood, Obama offers people a chance to see Kennedy in a new light and to better understand who he was as a person. Obama is able to praise and memorialize Kennedy by discussing the qualities that made him a great man.*

This example expands on the previous one by connecting the rhetorical device to the rest of the speech and offers more specific analysis on why Obama included the personal anecdote.

To get a good score on this type of essay, you must go beyond just naming the rhetorical device. You have to answer the why and the how. Make sure that every rhetorical and literary device you include in your essay is connected back to the author's purpose. Make the connections clear.

Summary:

- The goal of this type of essay is to identify the author's purpose and how it is achieved.
- Don't write a critique of the text or say whether you agree/disagree with the author/speaker.
- Flatter the test-writers by emphasizing what the author did well.
- Use SOAPS to find the context and other relevant details.
- Identify 3–4 rhetorical/literary devices and focus on only one per body paragraph. One device can be discussed in multiple paragraphs if it is used in different ways.
- Use quotes to help support your thesis and cite if necessary.
- Include an analysis of each device that answers why the author chose it and how it supports the author's purpose.

Next Steps:

- ❏ Plan your "fill-in-the-blank" thesis statement, transitions, and template in advance.
- ❏ Practice using SOAPS and memorize what the acronym stands for.
- ❏ Learn the rhetorical devices that may appear in your prompt.

Chapter 12

Synthesis

Applicable to: AP Art History, AP European History, AP U.S. History, AP World History: Modern, AP English Language and Composition, AP French/German/Italian/Spanish Language and Culture, AP Japanese Language and Culture, AP Latin, AP Spanish Literature and Culture, TOEFL, ACT

Goals

In this chapter, you will learn how to:

- use a chart to identify similarities and differences in the provided sources
- use multiple sources within a single, cohesive body paragraph
- synthesize multiple points of view to demonstrate complexity

TOO MUCH INFORMATION!

Essay prompts that provide multiple documents, passages, or viewpoints (which we will simply call "stimuli" in this chapter) can be overwhelming. Not only do you have to understand each one, but you also have to incorporate some or all of them into your essay in addition to having a solid organizational structure and an overarching thesis. In this chapter, we'll take a look at the two most important skills to master when it comes to synthesizing (which means "putting together") multiple stimuli: making connections between the different stimuli and smoothly incorporating them into a cohesive essay.

LET'S MAKE A CONNECTION

Whether your essay contains documents, passages, or viewpoints, it's a good idea to begin by writing notes as you look through them. If your essay asks you to take a stance on an issue, note whether each stimulus is "for," "against," or "neutral" toward the issue. You could also jot down a quick note about the perspective each one is taking. Some documents may offer more than one perspective; for instance, a text could discuss the benefits of something in one paragraph and the drawbacks in another paragraph. In that case, label each paragraph or portion of the text instead of the text as a whole.

No matter which test you are taking, you'll be given some kind of question in addition to the provided stimuli. Keep the question in mind as you are looking through the materials you have been given. Underline or circle key words that relate to the question to allow you to make connections to what you will eventually be answering. For instance, if the question asks about a certain time period or event, you could note whether each document was written before, during, or after. If the question asks you to analyze a certain theme in multiple passages, make sure to note that before you begin reading. That way, you can use your time efficiently by marking instances of that theme while you are reading the passages.

 Note the topic you are being asked about, and look for elements of the stimuli that relate to that topic while you are examining them.

IT'S ALL ABOUT THE PLAN...AGAIN

In this book, we've emphasized the importance of having a plan before you write. As overwhelming as essays that require you to synthesize can be, you'll find the process much easier if you spend some time planning beforehand. This will look different depending on what kind of essay you are taking, so let's take a closer look at some specific types of essays.

Document-Based Questions

For AP History Document-Based Questions (DBQs) and the AP English Language Synthesis essay, you'll be given 6–7 documents that could include texts, graphs, and/or images that provide different perspectives. Your documents will likely take up several pages, and it can be difficult to juggle all of them in your mind. After you have underlined key words and jotted down the viewpoints that the documents take, you may find it helpful to group the documents into a chart. Here's how a simple chart could look for a prompt with six documents related to wind turbines:

For	Against	Neutral
B	B	A
D	C	
F	E	

As you are formulating your viewpoint, your chart will help you to see where the support is for each side. You can also make your chart more elaborate by adding some brief notes:

For	Against	Neutral
B – clean, renewable	B – noisy, unreliable	A – picture of wind turbine
D – good for economy	C – disruptive noise	
F – efficient, cheap	E – ugly	

Adding these quick notes will help you to draw connections among the documents. For instance, two of them describe wind turbines as loud, so you could compare those two documents to see how the details they provide are similar or dissimilar. Source E focuses on the look of wind turbines, so you can use Source A, an image of a wind turbine, to identify the visual features it discusses. The arguments given in favor of wind energy are diverse, so you have several points of view to work with if you want to take that approach in your argument.

Essays with Fewer Stimuli

You can use a similar method for organizing your information on tests that provide only two or three sources with differing viewpoints, such as many of the AP Language Exams, the ACT, and the TOEFL. In that case, you will not have as many different stimuli to include in the chart, but it may still be helpful to group together any that provide similar or related views.

Comparing Texts

For essays that require you to compare only two texts or works of art, such as on the AP Art History, AP Latin, and AP Spanish Literature Exams, you'll want to organize your ideas differently. As we mentioned before, the question you are given will provide a certain theme or lens through which you are being asked to compare the two works. After you have identified where each work exhibits that theme, you may find it helpful to make a chart showing similarities and differences. Here's how that could look for a prompt with two passages, where the question asked about the fighting strategies that were described.

Passage 1	Passage 2	Both
–attacked while foraging	–attacked while marching	–involve an ambush
–hit-and-run tactic	–feigned retreat strategy	
–Caesar saved troops	–loss of many soldiers	

By noting an overall similarity in the texts, you have a main focus for your essay, and the differences can be discussed and compared in your body paragraphs.

FITTING IT ALL IN

Once you have grouped the viewpoints or jotted down similarities and differences, it's time to decide on your thesis. First, take another look at what the question is asking. In our wind turbine example from earlier, the question did not ask whether wind turbines are good or bad: instead, it asked about the key considerations in deciding whether or not to build a wind farm. If you are only looking at the documents, you can easily misinterpret what you are being asked to do, and if your thesis statement does not address the question, you'll score poorly.

Your thesis must respond to what the question is asking—not simply what you notice when comparing the documents.

Once you have settled on your thesis statement, decide which of the stimuli you will use and how they relate to your point of view. If your prompt only provides two or three items, you will need to use both/all of them. However, for essays that provide 6–7 documents, you will be told how many you need to incorporate, at a minimum. Either way, consider how each relates to your thesis statement. If it directly supports your thesis statement, plan to include that document. If it provides a counterargument, consider how you could incorporate the document to either dismiss the argument or use it to qualify your point of view. Only exclude a document if you can truly see no way that it can relate to your argument, as you can often score higher for including more documents.

As you consider how the stimuli relate to your thesis, start to plan out your body paragraphs. Let's see how that might look for the wind turbine example from earlier. Remember, your essay will likely have an introduction and a conclusion in addition to these body paragraphs.

Body Paragraph 1: Potential benefits → Sources B, D, and F

Body Paragraph 2: Potential drawbacks → Sources B, C, E, and A
(since A relates to E)

Alternatively, you could focus each body paragraph on a different consideration.

Body Paragraph 1: Noise → Sources B and C

Body Paragraph 2: Economics → Sources D and F

Body Paragraph 3: Appearance → Sources E and A

As you can see, the chart makes it much easier to notice similarities that allow one paragraph to reference multiple documents.

For the comparison essays we discussed earlier, you could organize your essay as such:

Body Paragraph 1: How the first work exhibits the theme

Body Paragraph 2: How the second work exhibits the theme

Body Paragraph 3: Similarities and differences

Here's another option:

Body Paragraph 1: Context for the works and their theme

Body Paragraph 2: Similarities in how the two works relate to the theme

Body Paragraph 3: Differences in how the two works relate to the theme

You can come up with your own organizational strategy, as long as each body paragraph has a clear focus and you address all parts of the question.

ADDRESSING THE OTHER SIDE

Students often struggle to incorporate multiple points of view in argumentative essays. After all, if your thesis is that something is good, why would you want to include an argument saying that it's bad? Well, the whole reason many of these essay prompts provide multiple perspectives is to test you on your ability to understand complexity.

Have you ever heard a commercial for a product and thought it sounded too good to be true? You might have been wondering, "What's the catch?" A one-sided essay leaves the reader with the same question. If the topic were so simple that only one side needed to be included, the test-writers wouldn't have asked the question. If you have ever seen a commercial that addressed your concerns, you probably found it much more convincing. For instance, the speaker informing you that the product was non-toxic for pets could answer a question you might have. This is an example of dismissing a possible objection. Here is how that could look in an essay about whether technology is beneficial or problematic:

> *Some may argue that technology removes the human element, but technology can connect people from all over the world, which actually humanizes people's lives more.*

This example references an alternative point of view but disputes the basis of the counterargument in favor of the author's thesis.

Alternatively, a commercial could give a concession. For instance, it could state that the product is toxic to pets. This does not necessarily mean the product is bad, but it simply shouldn't be used by people who have pets. Let's see how a concession can work in an essay.

> *It's true that technology is less human. However, there are benefits to removing the human element. Humans are biased and make mistakes, while technology can treat all people fairly and reduce harmful errors.*

This example acknowledges an alternative point of view but uses that viewpoint to strengthen the argument. Here's another way to address the opposition:

> *While technology has many benefits, it does unfortunately remove the human element from many interactions. However, the ways that technology can help us vastly outweigh this drawback; we can interact with humans in other ways, and machines can allow us to have more free time in order to do so.*

This concession acknowledges the validity of a differing viewpoint, but it argues that the opposing view does not weaken the author's thesis.

Regardless of how you choose to relate opposing viewpoints to your thesis, it's crucial that you do so. Many rubrics explicitly state that they want to see complexity in your essay, and addressing multiple ways of looking at the issue will help you earn a top score in that area.

We'll conclude by emphasizing one of the most important points for synthesis essays.

💡 The stimuli are used to support the points that you are making. Be sure that you do not merely summarize what has been provided.

As with any essay, make sure that each body paragraph has a focus. You may reference multiple stimuli in one body paragraph, but be sure that each has a clear role in how it relates to your thesis. If you merely summarize each of the stimuli and don't draw clear connections between or among them, you will not receive a good score.

Summary:

- Start by understanding the question, as it is the lens through which you should examine the stimuli you are provided.
- Note key words from the question in the stimuli, and jot down the main point of each one.
- Use a chart to identify similarities and differences.
- Plan the focus of each body paragraph and how you will use one or more stimuli in them.
- Find ways to incorporate multiple points of view to add complexity.

Next Steps:

- ❐ Use sample prompts to practice making a chart to identify points of view or similarities and differences.
- ❐ When making an argument, ask yourself, "What concerns might someone have about this?" in order to determine how to address the other side.

Chapter 13

Argumentative Essays

Applicable to: AP Comparative Government and Politics,
AP European History, AP U.S. History,
AP World History: Modern, AP U.S. Government and Politics,
AP English Language and Composition,
AP English Literature and Composition, AP French/German/
Italian/Spanish Language and Culture,
AP Japanese Language and Culture, TOEFL, ACT

Goals

In this chapter, you will learn how to:

- come up with a strong argument
- support your point of view with reasoning and examples
- organize an argumentative essay effectively

PICK A SIDE

One type of long essay found on standardized tests is the argumentative essay. This type of essay tests your ability to formulate an argument and support it with evidence and reasoning. Because this is a long essay, having a plan is essential to getting a good score. The prompts for argumentative essays allow for different kinds of arguments, which means that you have a lot of options as to what you will write. However, this plethora of possible arguments can also lead to problems if you don't plan. One of the worst things to happen on an argumentative essay is that you start the essay arguing one side of the topic and end up advocating for the other side by the end of the essay. This is a common occurrence when you simply start writing without using any time to prewrite. Even if you change your mind while writing, don't change your argument. Stick with your original argument throughout your essay. In order to get a good score, take the time to come up with your argument, select your evidence, and outline the basic structure of your essay.

Agree to Disagree

To write a good argumentative essay, you need to have a good argument.

 An argument is a defensible claim that is supported with reasoning and evidence.

Let's take a look at some statements that are NOT arguments to get a sense of what to avoid, and then we'll see some examples of good arguments. We'll give you examples from two areas, one responding to a prompt about what caused the French Revolution and another, more open-ended one asking whether people should explore the unknown.

> *The French Revolution had many causes.*

> *There are some benefits and some drawbacks to exploring the unknown.*

Is it possible to disagree with these statements? No, you can't argue that the French Revolution did not have many causes because that's not how history works. Likewise, you can't argue against a statement that says there are good and bad aspects to something. These statements are vague and are not arguments.

In my opinion, economic depression was the main cause of the French Revolution.

I like exploring unknown things.

We're getting closer to arguments with these statements, but there are still issues. On the surface, they look like arguments because you can support them with examples. You could write an essay looking at how economic depression caused the French Revolution or an essay that includes examples of unknown things you liked exploring. However, both of these statements are phrased as opinions, which are not arguments. You cannot meaningfully argue with someone's opinion; for example, the opposing point of view to the second example above would be *No, you don't like exploring unknown things*, which isn't really a valid disagreement.

An argument must be something that can be disagreed with.

The French Revolution was a period of social unrest.

Many people view the idea of exploring the unknown with trepidation.

Can you disagree with these statements? No, because they're statements of facts. You cannot argue with facts, so you cannot base your argumentative essay on a fact.

> *Three of the main causes of the French Revolution were economic inequality, the growing popularity of Enlightenment ideas, and poor harvests.*

> *Exploring the unknown can be terrifying, but overcoming that terror leads to personal growth, regardless of the unknown entity itself.*

How would you disagree with these statements? For the first one, you could argue a different set of main causes for the French Revolution. For the second one, you could argue that exploring the unknown has primarily negative consequences, not positive ones. These statements are good arguments because they both make a claim and provide reasoning and evidence for it. Also, it's clear to the reader what the essay will be about.

> When you are planning your argumentative essay, make sure you have an argument before you start writing. This will ensure that you have a direction for your essay and that you are appropriately responding to the prompt.

History and Government APs, Specifically

While many of the argumentative essays are more open and creative and thus allow more flexibility in the thesis statements, the AP Exams for History and Government have more specific requirements for their thesis statements. Let's take a look at those specifics.

An argumentative essay prompt for one of the history tests may ask you evaluate the extent to which an event influenced or marked a turning point in various areas of society or a relationship and how things were the same or different before and after the event. Unacceptable thesis statements do not fully address the prompt or simply restate the prompt. Note that these typically ask for *the extent* of the impact, which you can think of as *how* or *in what ways* the event had an effect.

The prompt asks about the extent to which World War I caused the ratification of the Nineteenth Amendment.

> 🙁 World War I had a large impact on women's role in society. 🙁

This thesis only partially answers the question, as it does not address the Nineteenth Amendment, so it would not earn a point.

> 🙁 World War I had a significant impact on the ratification of the Nineteenth Amendment. 🙁

This may seem like it answers the question, but the graders who work on the AP wouldn't give you a point for this thesis. It basically restates the prompt, which results in an argument that isn't very good.

> 😃 World War I affected the ratification of the Nineteenth Amendment, which granted women the right to vote, in that women were highly involved in the war effort. This involvement both showed the people in power that women's role in society was critical and left them with a desire to repay women by guaranteeing them additional rights. 😃

This is a good thesis because it explains *how* World War I caused the ratification of the Nineteenth Amendment.

> 😃 World War I had some effect on the Nineteenth Amendment but only because of women's massive efforts throughout the previous century in fighting for their rights; the war gave women more leverage, but female suffragists had already put the wheels in motion and in fact had already gained the right to vote in a number of states prior to World War I. 😃

It's fine to disagree with the prompt, as long as your argument is historically defensible. You can argue that the event in question was not a turning point (as long as you can prove how it wasn't!) or that it had a minor impact, in contrast to something else that had a more significant effect. AP graders are scoring on whether your thesis is written as an argument and whether it is historically defensible (so don't argue that the event had *no* impact, as that probably can't be defended).

For government tests, the prompt will likely ask you to make an argument about which type of some aspect of government is best for fulfilling a specific purpose. As with the other test types, your thesis statement must do more than restate the prompt.

> **The prompt asks whether sovereignty is best maintained through a democratic or an authoritarian form of government.**

An authoritarian form of government is best at maintaining sovereignty.

The AP graders don't give points to arguments like this one because the test-makers consider them to be merely restatements of the prompt.

Authoritarian governments maintain sovereignty more effectively because they have more power to act in their own interest, rather than that of their citizens.

A good thesis statement goes beyond the language given in the prompt. Not only do you need to take a stance, but your thesis also needs to identify the main line of reasoning you will be applying in your argument essay.

As emphasized elsewhere in this book, it is important to become familiar with the rubrics for all the tests you are taking so that you know what the graders are looking for in a thesis statement.

Right Side, Strong Side

One type of argumentative essay prompt is the open-ended question. These prompts do not provide perspectives on the question or offer sources of information. They may give you a quote that sets up the question, or they may simply give you a statement and ask why you agree or disagree with it.

These types of prompts can feel particularly challenging because they are so open. The important thing to remember is that there is no "right" answer to these questions. The graders are not looking for a particular argument or viewpoint; they are looking to see how well you can defend your argument. Additionally, don't be too concerned with writing what you believe in. If you have a stance on a particular argument, but during planning you can't come up with enough quality evidence to support it, it's time to change sides. Again, the graders aren't interested in whether you believe in your argument.

To come up with a good argument for open-ended prompts, it helps to start by brainstorming examples. As you come up with examples, you'll be able to see how you can make the strongest argument. To start, don't worry about the quality of the examples. Simply write a list or use a mind map to get the ideas flowing. As you look at your examples, you'll be able to see connections between them and the question. Your argument will flow out of your examples and the reasoning behind them. This can be very helpful if you don't have a strong opinion or immediate thought when reading the question.

Choose your argument based on how well you can support it.

Once you have your argument, don't forget to write a quick outline to organize where you'll discuss your examples. (As noted in the Long Essay Approaches chapter, an easy way to organize your essay is to use one example for each body paragraph.)

Different Sides to the Story

It can be tempting to look at the two or three options presented in the prompt and simply "pick a side." However, you will add complexity and sophistication to your essay if you can come up with a more complex point of view. Whether the prompt provides multiple perspectives or you're able to determine a few on your own, here are some ways you can use those differing viewpoints to construct a complex argument.

1. **Mix the perspectives.** One way to craft your own argument from different perspectives is to combine parts of the perspectives given into a new perspective.

Although this may seem counterintuitive, it can help you come up with a complex argument. To do this, first identify the perspective that agrees with the argument posed in the question and the perspective that disagrees with it. Let's see how this could work for a prompt about the effects of social media on friendships.

Pro: Social media helps people make friends because it allows people to easily share their lives with a large number of followers.

Con: Social media prevents people from forming friendships because people are not honest about themselves on social media.

To form your own argument, combine the argument from one of the perspectives with the reason from the other:

Social media prevents people from forming friendships because it allows people to easily share their lives with a large number of followers.

This argument shows complexity, which is a good thing to display in standardized essays and is explicitly scored in some rubrics.

2. **Undercut the Question.** Another way to make a complex argument is to question the question. The prompt will often focus on the tension in the relationship between two things or ideas. Although the prompt emphasizes the relationship, one way to come up with an argument is to question that relationship. For example, using the relationship discussed above between social media and making friends, you could question whether there is a relationship:

While the "social" in social media implies that it is used for connection, it does not mean that the purpose or goal of social media is to make friends.

Your essay could then go on to address the various points of view through this new lens.

3. **Find the Third Variable.** Similar to undercutting the question, the third variable looks at something that affects the question but is not addressed in the prompt. You may have encountered the phrase "correlation, not causation" in your science classes; this idea can help you when crafting a complex argument. For example, when discussing social media's effect on friendships, you could explore how time is a factor:

More time at school or work means there's less time for activities with friends. Since social media is fast and accessible, people are more prone to spend time on their phones.

Like with the open-ended prompts, your argument will need strong examples and evidence. A complex argument is not going to help you if you can't defend it.

THE DEFENSE RESTS

An argument is only as strong as the evidence that supports it. As you are coming up with your argument, you also want to think about what examples you can use to support it. Depending on the type of prompt and your ideas about it, you may think of your argument first or your examples first. There's not a right order to developing your thoughts; instead, focus on making sure your argument and your examples work together.

Your examples need to do more than relate back to your argument. Your examples are there for you to develop your reasoning, which in turn supports your argument. If you have an example that seems like a perfect fit but you are unable to articulate how it supports your argument, then it's not a good example. As you plan out your essay, it helps to include both the example and the reason that you'll explore in each of your body paragraphs.

Another thing to keep in mind as you build out your reasoning and examples is the particular subject of the test. For some tests, you'll be pulling examples from the content of the course. For history tests, you'll need to use historical events and documents. For literature, you'll be pulling from specific books you have read and the relevant plot and character details. The open-ended prompts allow you to bring in examples from other sources, like current events and your own personal experience. No matter the source of your examples, you'll want to be certain that your examples are specific and precise. Hypothetical examples are better than no examples, but they are typically too vague to earn you top marks.

For essays that require you to come up with your own examples, use academic examples wherever possible. Examples from history, literature, science, the law, psychology, and so on will help you sound like an expert more so than will examples from your personal experience, children's books, or pop culture. Think *To Kill A Mockingbird* or Marie Curie, not *Harry Potter* or TikTok. Of course, that's not to say that such examples can't be used; an amazing writer can make any topic work. However, less "serious" topics can make the writer seem silly, and while they won't ruin your score, you'll probably score higher by using more academic examples. That being said, a less serious example is better than no example at all, so if you absolutely can't think of anything more academic, use what you can come up with and don't waste too much time looking for other examples.

For more information about this, check out the chapter on Adding Outside Content.

TO BE FAIR

Throughout this chapter, we've talked about the importance of picking a side and defending it well. However, that doesn't mean that we ignore the other side of the argument. In fact, the test graders want to see complexity in your writing, and that means acknowledging the viewpoints and ideas that don't agree with your argument.

When writing your essay, you want to include the other side of the argument, but it shouldn't have equal weight or consideration. Instead, think of it like acknowledging a point but then dismissing it with your own evidence or reasoning:

The other side says this, but it fails to take into account this particular point that supports my argument.

Or

While the other side has this valid point, compared to the evidence of my argument, it is not the main reason for what happened.

You can also add complexity to your argument by including concessions or qualifications. This can include particular cases or situations where your argument may not apply or may not completely explain something. For instance, your argument could be that something from the prompt is harmful overall, but you may write an example to show a circumstance in which it is not harmful, which shows that you understand that the issue you have been given is complex and does not have a clear-cut "right" answer. The Synthesis chapter provides more information on combining multiple points of view.

When acknowledging and including points from the other side, it's vital that you are not equally supporting that side of the argument. As discussed in this chapter, you want to show that you have a strong argument with support. Giving equal weight to both sides of an issue or question will weaken your own argument and result in a lower score.

AND ANOTHER THING

Having a good structure for your essay is one way to make sure that your ideas and reasoning are coming through clearly. The Long Essay Approaches chapter included the classic 5-paragraph essay structure, but there is a specific model that you may find helpful to use for your body paragraphs in argumentative essays, called the Thesis-Antithesis-Synthesis or T-A-S model.

T-A-S MODEL FOR ARGUMENTATIVE ESSAYS

1. ▶ **Thesis:** Agrees with and supports the argument

2. ▶ **Antithesis:** Disagrees with and provides reasons against the argument

3. ▶ **Synthesis:** Combines reasons from the previous two paragraphs to arrive at a new perspective

Note that this type of essay should still have an intro and a conclusion; the structure above is for the body paragraphs in between. For the T-A-S model, your thesis statement will generally be placed either at the end of the Synthesis paragraph or in the conclusion. This structure is especially useful if you don't have a strong opinion on the topic or if your brainstormed examples don't clearly support one side over the other.

For example, suppose the argument is that money is "overrated." Your first body paragraph would explore support for this argument, such as psychological studies that show that wealthier people aren't necessarily happier. In the second body paragraph, you would explore reasons money isn't overrated, like the campaign for raising the minimum wage. Your third paragraph would synthesize those two viewpoints into a possible argument that money is overrated only when people have enough for their basic needs.

When writing your body paragraphs, like the rest of your essay, make sure your ideas and reasoning are clear. Each body paragraph should start with a topic sentence that lets the reader know what you will discuss. For the second and third body paragraphs, make sure to include a transition to avoid an abrupt switch from one viewpoint to another.

When including examples/evidence, make sure to set up each example beforehand and highlight the important aspects of it afterwards. For every example, think about why you are including it and how it supports your thesis statement, and then make sure that the answers to those questions are also clearly communicated to the reader. End each body paragraph by connecting back to the thesis statement.

If you have a lot of support/examples for your argument, you may want to spend more of your essay focused on your particular argument. If that is the case, you can save the counterargument for the last of your three body paragraphs:

1. **Support:** First example/evidence in support of your argument

2. **Support:** Second example/evidence in support of your argument

3. **Counter:** Introduce counterargument and then refute it; include third example/evidence

Another way to structure your essay is to think about the connections between your examples and how they build on each other. If you have a solid argument and your examples support it well, then there is a good chance that your examples will also help support each other. You can then structure your essay by putting them in an order that makes sense and helps convince the reader of your argument. As mentioned elsewhere, you can think of your essay as taking the reader on a journey.

With an argumentative essay, the journey should help the reader see the value of your argument.

Let's go back to the example thesis statements from earlier. For the French Revolution example, the body paragraphs are clear-cut. The thesis included three causes of the French Revolution, so each body paragraph would be centered on how that event or circumstance was a main cause of the French Revolution. The essay about exploring the unknown offers more flexibility. Let's see that thesis statement again:

Exploring the unknown can be terrifying, but overcoming that terror leads to personal growth, regardless of the unknown entity itself.

There are many ways the body paragraphs of this essay could be structured. Here are three possibilities (remember that each one would have an introduction and a conclusion paragraph as well):

BP1: An explanation and examples of unknown things

BP2: An explanation of why unknown things can be terrifying

BP3: An explanation and examples of personal growth that can result from overcoming terror

---

BP1: The beginning of one example of how someone overcame terror of an unknown thing

BP2: The middle of that same example

BP3: The end of that extended example, explaining how the person grew

---

BP1: Example of someone overcoming terror of an unknown thing and achieving personal growth

BP2: Second example of someone overcoming terror of an unknown thing and achieving a different kind of personal growth

BP3: Concession paragraph showing an example of where someone should not have explored the unknown

———————————————

Any of these formats, or many others, could effectively support the author's argument. If you'd like, decide on your own plan or template before test day so that you don't have to waste time determining your essay's structure.

No matter which essay structure you use, it's important that you plan and outline before writing so that your argument is persuasive.

Summary:

- Pick a side of the argument and stick with it throughout the essay.
- A good argument is a defensible claim supported by reasoning and evidence. Avoid statements of personal preference or opinions as well as statements that don't take a side.
- Make sure your argument addresses all parts of the prompt.
- For open-ended questions, brainstorm examples and choose an argument that you can support before beginning to write.
- You can create a complex argument by mixing perspectives, undercutting the question, or looking at a third variable.
- Strong examples provide good reasoning for your argument.
- Acknowledge the other side of the argument in your essay.
- Structure your essay in a way that showcases your reasoning and evidence.

Next Steps:

- ☐ Practice writing an argument: a thesis statement that can be disagreed with.
- ☐ Decide what structure you will use for your argumentative essay.
- ☐ Using sample prompts, practice coming up with examples to support your point of view, if applicable to your test type.

Chapter 14
Personal Essays

Applicable to: ISEE, SSAT

Goals

In this chapter, you will learn how to:

- show your personality in the best light
- show the admissions office your writing skills
- prepare and incorporate examples
- make your essay stand out

An essay type that is less common on standardized tests is the personal essay. However, even if you are not taking the SSAT or the ISEE, you will almost certainly have the experience of writing a personal essay for your college applications, and some of the tips and strategies in this section will help with that essay (though you will have much more time to write your college essay!). Let's take a look at how to approach personal essays.

YOU'RE THE STAR!

The main way these essays differ from the other ones in the book is that they are about you as a person. Even an essay that asks you to take a stance on an issue is not really about you; it's about your ability to defend an argument. With a personal essay, your goal is to let the reader know about you as a person. After all, this essay is being used for admission to a school, so this is your opportunity to show the admissions officers who you are beyond what is shown in your grades, application, and recommendations.

At the same time, a simplistic "all about me" essay won't do. The personal essay is not only an opportunity to let the admissions office know about your personality, but it is also a chance to show off your academic skills, such as vocabulary, knowledge of proper English, and ability to organize your ideas. Thus, your two goals in a personal essay are to highlight your writing skills and to help the admissions office get to know your personality.

PERSONAL ESSAY GOALS

1. ▶ Show off your writing abilities.

2. ▶ Let the reader see your personality and what's important to you.

ADVANCE PLANNING HELPS

Most personal essay prompts are not "yes or no" questions; rather, they typically ask you to write about your own idea or experience. For instance, you may be asked to write about a person you admire, a meaningful experience, or a time you faced and overcame a challenge. It might be intimidating to think of having to quickly come up with a topic on test day, especially considering you won't have much time to write your essay. The good news is that you can do some advance planning. Prior to test day, jot down some important aspects of your life that you could write about if they were relevant to the prompt. Try to come up with the following:

- ❑ Several people you admire or who have influenced you: one real person in your life, one person from history, and one fictional book character

- ❑ An experience that shaped who you are

- ❑ Something in your life that you are passionate about (preferably something academic- or community-oriented—not video games or sleeping)

- ❑ A challenge or obstacle you overcame

Most likely, your essay prompt will be broad enough to allow you to write about one of these, even if it doesn't ask about these exact topics. For instance, let's say one of your prepared topics was a school trip to New York City that was a formative experience for you. If instead the prompt asks about a place that is special to you, perhaps you could write about New York City, which is special to you because of that formative experience. Or, perhaps you prepared to write about your passion for playing soccer. If the prompt asked about an event you look forward to each year, you could write about an annual soccer tournament. When you write down these potential essay topics, spend some time considering how you could write about each one if you are able to use it in the prompt you receive. For instance, think about the important points that you would want to make sure to get across in your essay.

The Spirit of the Prompt, Not the Letter

Remember, your goals here are to write a great essay and to show your personality. Your goal is not to answer the question "correctly." The admissions officers are not primarily going to judge your essay by how closely it aligns with what the question was asking. Use a topic that is close enough to the prompt, even if it doesn't answer it exactly, as in the examples we just mentioned. You are much better off writing a fantastic essay that is very close to what the question asked than writing an essay that is exactly what the question asked but doesn't make a strong impact, either because you had to determine your topic very quickly and went with something that was just okay or because you took so long to find a great topic that you didn't have enough time to write in detail.

Prepare some quality topics in advance that can apply to a wide variety of prompts, and then try to make one of those subjects fit with the prompt you are given.

Remember, you can also plan out the structure of your essay in advance. Before test day, determine what your essay template will be. On test day, jot down your thesis statement and the focus of each body paragraph before you begin writing. See the chapter on Long Essay Approaches for more on these advance-planning techniques.

FOLLOW SOME RULES BUT BREAK OTHERS

Like with the other essays in this book, your personal essay should employ proper punctuation, grammar, and spelling as much as possible. However, this is one essay that can, and probably should, break some of the other essay rules we discussed earlier. This is because one of your two goals here is to showcase your personality. A dry, academic essay doesn't fulfill this aim (hopefully!). For this essay, don't be afraid to let your personality show through. Humor and even sarcasm can be great ways to do so, if those are aspects of who you are. Or, if you are an extremely passionate person, let the reader see that! Don't be afraid to show your true self and be honest.

On the other hand, remember that this essay is a component of the admissions process. Don't write your essay about an experience or passion of yours that could be perceived as silly or unimportant, such as the fact that you typically lie on the couch and watch TV after school or how it felt when you received the headphones you wanted for your birthday, for example. Likewise, if your essay focuses on the fact that you tend to oversleep and procrastinate, you're not going to look so great to the readers. If you are writing about your flaws, try to explain how you are working on those flaws or find a way to make them sound like they could be assets. Let's see some examples.

> *One flaw of mine is that I tend to get extremely angry and lash out at my family and friends when I don't get my way.*

This sounds babyish, and no school wants a student who behaves this way and doesn't seem to think it's a problem that can be fixed.

> *Throughout my life, I have found it challenging to overcome strong emotions. Whereas I used to lash out at family and friends when I didn't get my way, I have now found constructive ways to channel my anger, such as taking deep breaths, using logic, and removing myself from the situation to cool down.*

Everybody has flaws, and acknowledging those flaws shows self-awareness and maturity. By explaining how you have learned to combat and overcome those flaws, you will show the admissions officers that you are working to grow and improve as a person.

> *I always viewed it as a flaw that I can get angered easily. However, I've learned that anger can be a good thing if you use it in the right way. In recent years, I've become passionate about environmental issues. The anger I feel when I see the effects of the climate crisis fuels the passion with which I organize protests and write letters to my representatives.*

This example demonstrates personal growth, passion, and more about this student's personality, all of which are great.

Note that we aren't advising you to only show your good side. In fact, a candidate who doesn't seem to have any flaws could actually be suspicious! We all know no one is perfect, so mentioning your weaknesses can help show that you are a whole person with different sides. Just be sure to spin them in a positive light or balance them with your strengths.

On a related note, just as it's fine to use humor in a personal essay, casual language is more acceptable. That's not to say that you should write "b/c" instead of "because" or use hashtags (please don't do either of those!), but contractions (like "it's" instead of "it is") and slightly less formal constructions can be okay here.

FOCUS ON THE TWO GOALS

An aspect of this type of essay that can be tricky is knowing what level of detail to use. If you are writing about a character from a book, it can be tempting to write about everything that happens to that character. Or, if you are telling about a personal experience, you may find it challenging to know which details are important to include and which should be left out.

Remember, your goals are to write a great essay and show your personality. You should only include details that help further those goals. For the examples above, you should only include details about the characters and events that either 1) help provide background information so that the reader knows what you're talking about, or 2) support your answer to the question, also known as your thesis statement.

Let's see an example body paragraph.

The prompt asked about a person from literature with whom you identify.

One way I identify with Guy Montag from <u>Fahrenheit 451</u> is that he learns to question the principles he was raised with. As a fireman in his society, his role is to burn banned books. At first, he doesn't question this, but after being influenced by his young, free-thinking neighbor Clarisse, he begins to wonder whether the books truly should be burned. Reading the books furthers his newfound conviction that his society's mandate is oppressive and misguided. By questioning his earlier beliefs, Guy attempts to create a better life for himself and improve his society.

This paragraph is well-written and provides a good summary of the character's development in the book, but notice that it does not provide any information about the person who wrote it. This question is not really asking you to describe the character; it's asking you to use the character to reveal aspects of your own personality. Let's see a better example.

One way I identify with Guy Montag from <u>Fahrenheit 451</u> is that he learns to question the principles he was raised with. While he initially does not question his societal role as a book-burning firefighter, he is later spurred by his young, free-thinking neighbor Clarisse to investigate whether the books truly merit being destroyed. For me, it didn't take long to begin questioning my world; ever since I was small, my parents would become exasperated by my constantly asking them, "Why?" As a recent example, I was frustrated by my school's policy that male students could not have long hair. The school administration admitted that it did not have a solid reason for this sexist ban, so several of my classmates and I were able to convince the administrators to change the policy so that all students could wear the styles they prefer. Just as Guy learned that laws don't always reflect what is right and wrong, by constantly questioning the world around me, I've developed a critical eye that helps me identify instances of injustice.

This paragraph uses the literary example as a jumping-off point to discuss an aspect of the author's personality, which is exactly what you want to do. The author here provides some details about the character so that the reader can understand the connection being made, but most of the paragraph focuses on the writer's personality. This person also took the opportunity to share an example that highlights his or her leadership abilities, which could be appealing to admissions officers. If you have prepared in advance a character you could write about, as we discussed earlier, you'll be able to cite the book title, character's name, and some important details, which shows your academic skills as well.

MAKE IT INTERESTING!

As we said earlier, these essays are less formal, and your essay will do more for you if you can grab the reader's attention or even entertain the admissions officers.

Let's see some ways you can make your essay more interesting.

1. **Use stories.** Narratives can both give you something concrete to write about and hold the attention of the reader. They can also be a great way to *show* aspects of your personality rather than simply *telling* about them. Just remember not to get carried away with the details; everything you write should tie back to your overall goals, not fill your essay with fluff. Details that help paint a picture are great, but don't include events that aren't directly related to your point.

2. **Add a rhetorical question.** Questions reach off of the page and make a connection with the reader. Here's an example: *My history teacher offered the class 10 points of extra credit if we interviewed an older relative. Seems like a pretty sweet deal, right?* These sentences invite the reader to step into the writer's shoes, and the question foreshadows that the assignment might not have gone as expected, which makes the reader want to keep going. This is also an example of where casual language is okay, as it reveals insight into what the author might have been thinking and furthers the personal connection.

3. **Inject humor.** Take a look at the following examples: 1) *In fifth grade, I decided to play percussion, and I have been taking band class ever since.* 2) *Much to the dismay of my family members, I chose to play percussion beginning in the fifth grade, and they have been wearing earplugs ever since.* Which example is more interesting? The second one! These sentences provide essentially the same meaning, but the second example adds humor and sensory details that make a stronger impression. Don't be afraid to exaggerate slightly for comedic effect. Making fun of yourself a little bit can also help the reader feel empathy and make a stronger connection.

DON'T NEGLECT PROPER ORGANIZATION

No matter your topic, your essay must be organized into multiple paragraphs. It isn't an absolute necessity that this essay have an introduction and a conclusion, although you certainly can organize your essay into the typical 5-paragraph style if you'd like to (see the Long Essay Approaches chapter for more on organization). The most important thing is that you do not just write one long, rambling paragraph. Decide on the focus of each paragraph before you start writing, and end the paragraph when you are finished writing about that topic. For instance, in our *Fahrenheit 451* example from earlier, the paragraph is focused on one aspect of Guy's personality with which the writer identifies. This essay would have one or two other paragraphs that describe additional personality traits the writer wants to highlight, and it would have some kind of beginning and ending—these could be distinct introduction and conclusion paragraphs or just a sentence in the first paragraph that introduces the point of the essay and a sentence at the end of the last paragraph that sums it up.

Whether you start with an introduction or not, be sure to make your thesis statement clear. Since this essay isn't being scored, the thesis statement isn't as important as it is for some of the other essays in this book, but this statement makes it clear to the reader what you'll be focusing on. Your thesis statement is basically your answer to the question that was asked, and it may include a preview of the points or examples you'll be using. Here are some example thesis statements:

> *I identify with Guy Montag from Fahrenheit 451 because of his willingness to question what he was taught and because of his courage in choosing a different path.*

> *One place that is special to me is New York City because it was there that I learned the true power of friendship.*

> *Since I love playing soccer, an event I look forward to every year is the interscholastic soccer tournament in my city.*

As you can see, the thesis statement does not have to be elaborate, but it will let the reader know right away *why* you are writing about the topics in your essay.

Summary:

- Focus on two goals: Showing off your writing skills, and letting the admissions officers know who you are and what's important to you.
- Prepare some versatile topics in advance.
- Use proper English, but don't be afraid to be less formal at times if it makes the essay more interesting.
- Organize your essay into paragraphs and have a beginning, middle, and end.

Next Steps:

- ☐ Plan some topics that you could use on test day for a variety of prompts.
- ☐ Using sample prompts, write some practice essays for a school counselor or other adult to read.

Chapter 15
Foreign Language Essays

Applicable to: AP Chinese Language and Culture,
AP French/German/Italian/Spanish Language and Culture,
AP Japanese Language and Culture,
AP Spanish Literature and Culture, TOEFL

Goals

In this chapter, you will learn how to:

- go beyond the basics and impress the graders
- incorporate culture into your essay
- approach written or spoken source materials
- write appropriately for your audience

Many of the other chapters in this book provide information that applies equally well to foreign language essays. For instance, whether your essay is in English or not, it must be well-organized and have a beginning, middle, and end. Regardless of the language, your essay should use appropriate vocabulary and varied sentence structures. Let's take a look at some aspects of foreign language essays that make them slightly different from the other essays in this book.

SWEAT THE SMALL STUFF

Many of the other essays in this book do not explicitly grade you on the correctness of your punctuation, grammar, and spelling. Those things matter, but mainly to the extent that they help make the meaning of your essay clear. If you make grammar errors but the grader can still understand what you are trying to say, those errors likely won't significantly hurt your score.

Language essays, on the other hand, explicitly score you on mechanics, which shouldn't be a surprise. The graders want to see that you can write an essay, but the essay in most cases is really a way for the test writers to assess your ability to communicate in the language. While top-scoring essays can still have some errors, incorrect grammar and usage will hurt your score, so you should attempt to minimize mistakes as much as possible. Of course, part of that means paying close attention and working hard in your course to improve your language skills as much as possible. However, on test day, it will also be important to carefully read over your work prior to the end of the allotted time to ensure that you have found and corrected any errors that you are capable of fixing. As with the other tests in this book, errors that impede understanding are the most problematic; minor spelling and punctuation errors won't hurt your score as much, but you should still try to write correctly as much as possible.

KNOW THE COMMON MISTAKES

In your course, your teacher has likely highlighted and spent a lot of time going over some of the areas that are particularly challenging in that language. For instance, gender in a foreign language can be difficult for native English speakers because most English words don't have a gender. Native Russian speakers may struggle with English articles because their native language does not use articles. Every language presents its own challenges, whether they are word order, tense, gender, accents, or any number of other features, depending on the native language of the person learning it.

Learn what mistakes are commonly made in your foreign language by people who speak your native language so that you'll be able to watch for those errors.

SHOW OFF!

A basic essay with simple vocabulary and sentence structures will do the job, but it may not earn you a high score. The scorer is not simply looking for you to write a basic response to the question. Remember, the goal of these essays is to determine your skills in the language. The prompt gives you a broad focus of what to write about, but don't simply fulfill the requirements of the prompt and call it a day. To earn a good score, you'll need to include lots of details, vary your sentence structure, and incorporate vocabulary and more challenging grammar formulations. For instance, the Spanish subjunctive is notoriously difficult, so if you are able to use it effectively, you'll impress the grader (though don't try it if you're not sure it's correct, as you're better off with something that is correct but simple than something fancy but wrong). Likewise, irregular verbs can show that your knowledge of the language goes beyond the basic. Mastering the punctuation rules in the language of your test is another great way to impress the grader; different languages may use different types of quotation marks, format questions differently, or make different words capital or lowercase, for example.

It's important to use idioms correctly. For instance, if someone said in English "I arrived to the airport," you would instantly know that that person is not a native speaker. That's because we always say "arrived at," not "arrived to." There isn't any real reason for it, but that's just the way we say it. Every language has similar phrasings that can't be explained using broad rules. Thus, it's important to know not just vocabulary but also common phrases that include the words. You can't simply translate directly from English to the language your test is in (or vice versa if you are taking an English-language exam); you will need to know how various *ideas* are phrased in the language of your test, not just the direct translation of each word.

Speaking of vocabulary, you'll need a robust vocabulary for your essay (of course!). You can study vocabulary flashcards, but that isn't the only (or even the best) way to learn vocabulary. Reading books or articles at an appropriate level will expose you to new words in a textual context, which will help you both learn the meaning and learn how the word should be used, since as we just discussed, the idiomatic usage is just as important as the literal definition. A definition can only tell you so much; for instance, it could be said that "average" and "mediocre" are synonyms, but describing yourself as an "average student" compared with a "mediocre student" provides a different connotation (in the former, you're just typical, but in the latter, you're not very good).

In general, you are always better off correctly using a less fancy word than incorrectly using a complex vocabulary word, but to maximize your score, learn to use more advanced words in an appropriate way.

HOW CULTURED ARE YOU?

Most language courses teach you about the culture of the region in which the language is spoken in addition to how to read, speak, and write in the language. Assuming that you are learning the language to be able to read documents written by and converse with native speakers, it's important to understand those speakers' culture to better comprehend the information and communicate. Otherwise, you may be confused when a resident of Spain mentions going out for dinner at 10:00 P.M. or when a Latin text references public baths. In your essay, you may be able to refer to specific aspects of the culture that you have learned about, which can boost your score. Your ability to work this in will depend on the specific type of essay, but whenever possible, try to approach your essay as though you are a native speaker immersed in the culture, not a foreigner viewing it from afar.

GOING TO THE SOURCE

Many foreign language essay prompts will involve various sources, which may be articles, images, graphs, or spoken material. As you are reading a written source, jot down some notes for yourself on what is being said. You probably don't read as fluently in that language as in your native language, so having notes to refer to will save you time when you are composing your essay. If you come across a word that you don't know, try to use the context to figure it out. For instance, you may be able to use the topic to guess about what an unfamiliar word might mean. Or, it may sound similar to another word in that language or a similar one, which could help you guess about the root word. Keep in mind that if you were reading an article in your native language, there's a good chance that you might see a word you don't know or can't pronounce. That doesn't usually get in the way of your ability to understand the author's main points, so it shouldn't on a foreign language exam either. Don't panic or assume you won't be able to get a good score if there are some words you don't know; you simply need to understand the main ideas of the text in order to respond to it. If you are asked to translate a text and there is a word you don't know, simply take your best guess given the context. Remember, you can't lose points for wrong answers, and your score won't be significantly harmed if there are a few words you have to guess about.

For listening components, take good notes while you're listening. You probably won't catch every word, and that's okay. Focus on the speaker's main points. If the audio source is taking a stance on an issue, first try to determine and jot down what that stance is as well as the main lines of reasoning that are used so that you can incorporate them into your essay. If the recording is played a second time, at that point you can add more specific details to your notes. Of course, it will also help to spend a lot of time listening to the language through radio, TV and movies, and/or conversations so that you are used to hearing the language at the pace of speech.

TRY NOT TO CONFUSE OR OFFEND

If you were working at a store and a customer came up to you and said, "How are you feeling, baby?" you would probably feel a bit weirded out, because that person has spoken to you in a much more familiar way than is appropriate for strangers in a public setting. Instead, the person should have said something like, "Hi, how are you?" because that is what we consider to be appropriate in the United States. Likewise, if someone said, "Good day, how do you fare?" you'd probably give the person a confused side-eye because this greeting is overly formal and old-fashioned.

These English examples illustrate the importance of propriety. Without being cognizant of it, we all change our language according to the scenario. You speak one way with your friends, speak a different way with your teachers, and write another way for academic papers. For foreign language exams, it's important to know what is considered appropriate for the situation you will be writing in. For traditional essays, you should write in a formal, academic style, whereas for essays that include text messages and email exchanges with friends, you can use a more casual style (but you should still avoid slang that the grader may not be familiar with). It's critical to know what those styles mean for your language. For instance, going back to the examples from the previous paragraph, in the United States, it is completely normal to ask, "How are you?" in a greeting. However, in other countries, this would be odd and overly personal. As we discussed earlier, you cannot simply translate from your native language to the language of your test; make sure to know what phrases are appropriate in that language for a given scenario.

Language that is inappropriate for the situation can be confusing at best and offensive at worst.

Summary:

- Apply the overall strategies from other essays, but don't translate directly from your native language to the foreign language. Instead, learn the appropriate structures and idioms in that language.
- Make sure to use correct punctuation, grammar, and spelling as much as possible, as these skills count more on language exams than on other exams.
- Go beyond the basics and impress the graders with vocabulary words, advanced grammatical structures, and cultural references where possible.
- Jot down notes on the main idea of source materials, and don't worry if you can't figure out a few words. Your essay needs to incorporate the perspective or main idea of the source rather than the specific words.
- Aim to use a tone and register that are appropriate for the provided scenario.

Next Steps:

- ☐ Develop a robust vocabulary in your foreign language, including idioms.
- ☐ Learn some cultural tidbits about the people who speak your foreign language.
- ☐ Read and listen to a variety of sources in your foreign language so that you can learn appropriate ways of communicating to different audiences.

Chapter 16

Email Reply Writing

Applicable to: AP Chinese Language and Culture,
AP French/German/Italian/Spanish Language and Culture

Goals

In this chapter, you will learn how to:

- add details to strengthen your response
- use appropriate language and forms of address
- boost your score by adding cultural references, vocabulary, and/or varied sentence structures

Many AP Language Exams include a 15-minute email reply. No matter which language exam you are taking, they all ask for the same basic things: to address all questions and instructions in the prompt, to use appropriate language for the audience and event, and to write correctly. Let's take a closer look at these scoring areas; note that the examples are given in English here so that all test-takers will understand the points we are making in this chapter.

DO WHAT YOU'RE ASKED TO DO

The task itself may provide some specific instructions. For instance, it may ask you to include a greeting and a closing, use a certain form of address (such as formal or informal), and/or ask for additional details about something mentioned in the message. You may also see specific questions asked in the email itself.

In all cases, you need to be sure your response contains everything stated in the task and answers to any questions asked in the email.

To the extent that time allows, include details. Let's say that the original email asks why you are interested in attending an upcoming arts festival and what your accommodation needs are. Here are some sample responses to those questions:

> *I want to attend the festival because I like art, and I will need to stay in a hotel.*

This is better than not answering the questions at all, but this response won't earn you a top score. To do well, you'll need to elaborate. Note that everything in this conversation is made up, so you aren't being asked here to necessarily give information that is true about yourself (though you can do that if you would like to). Otherwise, just make up something that is within your writing abilities in the foreign language and makes sense in the context.

> 😃 *I would like to attend the festival because I am a journalist who reports on art. My newspaper has assigned me to write a story on your upcoming festival for the residents of my town. I do not like camping, so I would prefer accommodations in a hotel. I will need a bathroom with a shower as well as Wi-Fi access in order to communicate with my editor. I am also a vegetarian. Could you please tell me whether there will be food that is suitable for vegetarians?* 😃

This answer is much more detailed and shows more about your ability to communicate in the foreign language. It also addresses some aspects of the original email, which had mentioned camping and dining.

KEEP IT APPROPRIATE

An email also requires a greeting and a closing, whether that is explicitly stated in the task or not. This is one key element of your score on appropriate language: you must address the recipient properly. Typically, there is more than one acceptable way to do this, but make sure you consider whether your address should be formal or informal. In some cases, this is explicitly stated in the task; it may instruct you to use a formal form of address, for instance. If the tone is not explicitly stated, use relatively informal language if the email is stated as being from a friend or family member and more formal language if the email is from anyone else. Throughout the email, use appropriate pronouns and verb conjugations, where applicable, if the language you are writing in has both formal and informal versions.

Idiomatic language will boost your score, but you should avoid slang. To give some English examples, it would be appropriate to say "get rid of" or "let me know" or "right away," but it wouldn't be appropriate to describe something as "chill," "fire," or "legit."

💡 If you're not sure whether something is too casual, err on the side of being more formal.

Make sure that your greeting includes some form of "Dear [name]," with the person's title included as appropriate. Your email should end with some form of "Sincerely" and your name. Learn some common greetings and closings in the language of your test before you take the exam since this is guaranteed to be part of what you need to do.

Remember to be polite as well, especially if your email is replying to a person who is not supposed to be a friend or family member. Just as you would likely include "please" for requests in English, you should do the same in the foreign language, and thank the person as appropriate. Longer, explanatory sentences also sound more polite than brief, simplistic ones (such as *I need a hotel room*). Try to learn respectful phrases in your language prior to test day. For instance, consider the difference in English between saying *I want dumplings* and saying *I would like dumplings, please*. Most likely, the language you're studying has some forms that are more appropriate for polite conversations and requests.

USE YOUR WRITING SKILLS

Even though you will be writing in a foreign language, the English language paragraph-writing tips we've given you will still apply. For instance, you should vary your sentence structure (see the chapter on General Advice for more on that). Don't make your sentences overly simplistic, either. You're in an AP class, so your sentences shouldn't all be structured like the very basic sentences you learned to write in your first year studying the language.

Just like with English writing, you should vary your word choice as well. When possible, it's best not to use the same word more than once in the same sentence or repeat the same words in several successive sentences. Try to use synonyms so that you don't repeat the same words, just as you would in an English paragraph.

Use correct punctuation, grammar, spelling, and usage as much as possible. Not only are you being explicitly graded in this area, but mistakes in writing can make your email difficult for the grader to understand, which could harm your score. Be sure to write in the correct tense for the meaning you are trying to convey. See the chapter on Foreign Language Essays for more tips.

IT'S NOT JUST ABOUT BEING CORRECT

As we said earlier, if you are aiming for an above-average score, you'll need to write more than just a basic response to the prompt. Try to show off your knowledge of the language through the use of advanced or specialized vocabulary words and difficult tenses or constructions, where appropriate. However, if you are not certain of a vocabulary word, use a word you are sure you know instead, as it is worse to use a word incorrectly than to use a less fancy word.

Feel free to be creative in your response. The graders are not checking whether what you are saying is true (though don't be silly). If there is a certain topic or area for which you know a lot of related vocabulary, it may be a good idea to include that in your response, if applicable, so that you can show off your skills. These prompts tend to be fairly flexible, and they aren't looking for a single specific answer.

Include cultural tidbits wherever you can. In your class, you have learned about the culture of the location where the language you're studying is spoken—after all, this exam is called Language *and Culture*. Cultural references can help make your email stand out and show that you understand more than just the language's vocabulary and grammar. For instance, in the example from earlier, you could write that you look forward to eating *esquites* or *aligot,* or you could mention specific places you wish to visit in the city that the email originates from, if you are familiar with any.

Summary:

- Follow the instructions provided, and answer any questions from the email in the prompt.
- Add details, including cultural ones where possible.
- Use appropriate formal or informal structures depending on the prompt.
- Prepare some greetings and closings in advance.
- Use more advanced vocabulary and varied sentence structures to boost your score.

Next Steps:

- ❏ Memorize appropriate greetings and closings in your foreign language.
- ❏ Practice writing emails back and forth with friends who are studying the same language.

NOTES